**EVERYTHING YOU NEED TO KNOW
ABOUT SEX AND PURITY**

CHRISTIAN
SEX
ED

DANE FRAGGER

Christian Sex Ed: Everything You Need To Know About Sex and Purity
By Dane Fragger

Copyright 2020
All rights reserved.

Unless otherwise indicated, Scripture quotations are from the ESV® Bible (The Holy Bible, English Standard Version®), copyright © 2001 by Crossway, a publishing ministry of Good News Publishers. Used by permission. All rights reserved.

Cover design by DRU Creative Studio

Scripture quotations marked (KJV) are taken from the Holy Bible, King James Version (Public Domain).

Scripture quotations marked (MSG) are taken from THE MESSAGE, copyright © 1993, 2002, 2018 by Eugene H. Peterson. Used by permission of NavPress. All rights reserved. Represented by Tyndale House Publishers, a Division of Tyndale House Ministries.

Scripture quotations marked (NIV) are taken from the Holy Bible, New International Version®, NIV®. Copyright © 1973, 1978, 1984, 2011 by Biblica, Inc.™ Used by permission of Zondervan. All rights reserved worldwide. www.zondervan.com The "NIV" and "New International Version" are trademarks registered in the United States Patent and Trademark Office by Biblica, Inc.™

Scripture quotations marked (NKJV) are taken from the New King James Version®. Copyright © 1982 by Thomas Nelson. Used by permission. All rights reserved.

Scripture quotations marked (NLT) are taken from the Holy Bible, New Living Translation, copyright ©1996, 2004, 2015 by Tyndale House Foundation. Used by permission of Tyndale House Publishers, a Division of Tyndale House Ministries, Carol Stream, Illinois 60188. All rights reserved

ISBN: 978-0578635293

Printed in the United States of America

TABLE OF CONTENTS

INTRODUCTION

I had just finished having sex with a woman I hooked up with often. Instantly, something hit me. Something I'd never felt before. *Conviction.*

Immediately, I knew I had to let her go. So, there I stood, anxiously waiting and inwardly begging her to *please put on her clothes*. It was in that moment that I knew what Adam and Eve felt like in the garden of Eden after they sinned and tried to hide their nakedness from God.

I was naked.

She was naked.

I needed to hide from God.

And I needed her to put on her clothes!

When she finally did put both legs through her leggings, I blew a sigh of relief. I walked her downstairs, opened the garage and said, "I'll text you later." As soon as that garage door shut, I ran upstairs, went into the bathroom and jumped into the shower. The shower was the closest thing to a baptismal pool I could get to at the time. I had to wash *this sin* off me. I guess I hoped that the water shooting through the showerhead would grant me some spiritual cleansing.

That didn't work though.

Now, I was just a wet sinner. The conviction was there to stay.

That day, everything changed. Sex was no longer enjoyable. Neither were my late nights of watching porn, pursuing naked pictures or masturbating, because I knew hell was awaiting me. The reality of going to hell was crippling. So crippling that every night after I sinned sexually, I would cry out to the Lord with my hands lifted, "I'm sorry...I won't do it again."

But, I lied.

Beneath my fake repentance lurked a mind that was ready to sin again when, and if, given the right opportunity. Don't get me wrong—I wanted to desperately change. I just loved women too much to do so. However, even though my heart was burning for women, it was more afraid of burning in hell. That led me to make the hardest decision of my life: to kiss lust goodbye.

So I thought.

It was actually more like, "See you later." Nevertheless, for a short time after I was filled with God's spirit, I did give up my lustful pleasures. But since lust and I used to be one, she always knew how to lure me back in with her sweet nothings.

"Dane, you can have whatever you want," she said.

The thoughts—and mental pictures—of all that I could have made my mouth water.

Decisions. Decisions. Decisions.

Who do I make Lord over my life? Jesus or lust?

I believe that's the same question that is haunting this generation. Unfortunately, though, many have chosen the broad path and dove recklessly into the seas of lust. But no matter how deep you've sunk into the seas of lust, there's a great fisher of men named Jesus who can pull you out. If you're ready to be rescued, or learn about sex in an educational, scientific, transparent and—above all else—biblical manner, I invite you into my class, *Christian Sex Ed.*

101

THE BASICS

You can't escape it.
    You're surrounded by it.
    It's everywhere.
It's *sex.*

In an uncanny way, it has polluted our world. As a result of this, our society has become more sex-crazed and sexualized than ever before.

We know this to be true by:

1. **SEEING** how pornography has grown into a multi-billion-dollar industry, as well as a leading economic sector in U.S. entertainment.

2. **LISTENING** to the sexually suggestive music that objectifies women's bodies and glorifies immoral conduct against them.

3. **TURNING** on the television and noticing how the most popular shows are saturated with sensuality and nakedness. You can even find hints of lust and sexual undertones in children's television, too.

4. **LOOKING** at how the upcoming generation—Generation Z—is having sex for the first time at a younger age (16.62 years old) than any previous generation. That's a 1.11-year drop in the average age for virginity loss since the mid-90s. *See chart below.*

GENERATION	BIRTH YEAR	AVE. AGE VIRGINITY LOSS
Generation X	Mid-60s to Late-70s	17.84 years old
Millennial	Early-80s to Early-90s	17.73 years old
Generation Z	Mid-90s to Mid-2010s	16.62 years old
(Statistics provided by Christian Sex Ed Surveys) (950 Respondents)		

The list goes on, and only gets worse. And it's all because Satan and his demons are seducing and desensitizing our culture by making lustful things appear good and consequence-free.

Satan did something similar to Adam and Eve in the Garden of Eden. Through a serpent, he made what was forbidden look appealing, and the two ate the forbidden fruit. With Satan at his old tricks, this 21st-century generation has bitten the fruit. This time, it's lust. As the juice from this fruit drips down, our world's sexual purity goes down, corrupting the very thing that God made for good: *sex*. Therefore, since the enemy has infiltrated our society and twisted God's view of sex, we must start this discussion off by addressing the basic question: "What is sex?"

What is Sex?

The physical act of sex, also known as sexual intercourse, is when a man puts his erected penis into the vagina of a woman. As the penis enters, and intercourse begins, chemicals release throughout the body, charged to enhance the sexual experience. When the two finally reach the point of climax, the man ejaculates from his penis. The woman's vagina, anus and uterus contract as she orgasms.

I remember the first time I came to grips of that definition of sex. It wasn't during fifth-grade sex education like my friends and I hoped for. All that class gave us was a diagram of our body parts with definitions (like we didn't already know what we had) and a stick of deodorant. My understanding of sex didn't come through the small sex scene from the movie 8 Mile either. While the scene did strike a chord of curiosity, I couldn't fully comprehend what I saw. My mind was still innocent.

However, my real introduction to sex came a few weeks later. It was at a friend's house after school. He suggested we watch a video. I could tell by the tone of his voice that it wasn't something I was allowed to watch. I still agreed, though. He then scrolled through a few computer files until he found the video. Then, with a big grin, he turned around, looked at me, and hit play. To my complete shock, it was full-blown pornography. Like nothing I'd ever seen before. That was my crooked introduction to sex. [We'll discuss what transpired in 107: The Seed.]

Maybe you've had a crooked introduction to sex, too. Or, perhaps your view of sex has been skewed by the overwhelming lust in our society. Whether that be the case or not, it's essential that we get a clear picture of what God's plan was, and is, for sex. We can do this by first examining the Old Testament of the Bible and looking at the lives of the world's first two virgins.

The First Two to Ever Do It

It's no secret that Adam and Eve were the world's first virgins. They were also the first two to lose their virginity. A lot has changed since then, though. Therefore, I wonder what sex was like the first time for them? Did Adam know what to do or where to put it? Did God inform Adam on what to do? Was it part of Adam's instinct? Who initiated the sex? I'm going to go out on a limb and say that Adam initiated. I imagine that he woke up the first morning after being kicked out of the garden of Eden with something hard. Immediately, he looked at Eve and, from there, sex entered the world. It was through that moment, and their lives that we see God's plan and purpose for sex.

The first thing their lives show us is that God formulated sex for pleasure. When God created Adam and Eve, He created them with their reproductive organs. These organs yield great pleasure during sex.

Additionally, God uses sex as a means of populating the earth. In Genesis 1:28 (NIV), God said, *"Be fruitful and multiply..."* In other words, God was saying, "Have sex, have children and fill the earth." Sure, God could have created millions of people out of thin air, but He chose to start with one from the dust (Adam), the next from the rib (Eve), and the rest from a sperm and an egg through sex.

The final thing God shows through Adam and Eve is that sex is for the husband and wife *only*. Genesis 4:1 (NIV) says, *Adam made love to his wife Eve, and she became pregnant and gave birth to Cain.* He didn't make love to his side-chick, his girlfriend, his fiancée or his friend with benefits. He made love to his wife.

Then in Genesis 4:17, Adam and Eve's son, Cain, made love to his wife, and she became pregnant, too. If you noticed, the first two times in the Bible that sex is mentioned, it's only between a husband and wife. God didn't put these examples in Scripture by coincidence. Sex for the married was a part of His divine plan.

However, through the influence of lust and Satan, mankind eventually broke this plan and gave themselves over to different sexual sins. This left God no choice but to enforce rules regarding sex, such as: no sex outside of marriage; no sex with the same sex; no sex with animals; no sex with family members; no sex with another person's spouse; and no sex with a woman who is on her period (See Leviticus 18, Deuteronomy 22, and Numbers 25:1-9).

If you notice, there's one thing that wasn't on list: polygamous and concubine sex. Those acts seem rather ungodly to me. But, in the Old Testament, God allowed men to have multiple wives (Deuteronomy 21:15) and even concubines. There was a stipulation to this for kings, though. They could have more than one wife, but not "many" wives because their hearts would turn from God. Only God knows the number for "many" because Scripture doesn't tell us (Deuteronomy 17:17).

Nevertheless, although God allowed these men to engage in sex with multiple wives and concubines, it was still not His original plan or hope for sex! This is even more reason why we see God restoring His original plan for sex and marriage (Genesis 4:1) in the New Testament, where all sex outside of one husband and one wife is sin.

Sex in the New Testament

Scroll throughout the New Testament. You'll quickly discover at least twenty Scriptures that condemn sex outside of marriage. One particular passage makes it crystal clear that it's a sin:

> Now for the matters you wrote about: "It is good for a man not to have sexual relations with a woman. But since sexual immorality is occurring, each man should have sexual relations with his own wife, and each woman with her own husband."
> 1 Corinthians 7:1-2 (NIV)

This passage tells us a couple of things. First, it tells us that the members of the Church of Corinth (the church that Paul planted) had questions for the Apostle Paul regarding sex. Second, it tells us that someone from the Church of Corinth reported to the Apostle Paul that people were having sex outside of marriage.

It was this information that led the Apostle Paul to inform them that a man shouldn't have sex with a woman (outside of marriage). However, since this was happening, Paul says that each man should have sex with his own wife, and each woman have sex with her own husband. In this instruction to the Church of Corinth, Paul calls sex outside of marriage sexual immorality. He makes it clear that the only way to have sin-free sex is for it to be with your one spouse (of the opposite sex). That is God's perfect plan for sex.

Fornication:
Sexual intercourse between two people that aren't married to each other or pre-marital sex.
"Flee fornication." 1 Cor. 6:18 (KJV)

Class Wrap-Up

Even if you were to view pre-marital sex outside of the lens of Christianity, you can still see how sex is designed for one husband and one wife. Sex is emotional, vulnerable, spiritual and physical. Any act carrying that much weight should be done with someone who is spiritually and legally committed to you! Marriage fulfills both!

Therefore, it only makes sense to share something so special — sex — with someone who is committed to you in the safe place of marriage. In marriage, your body isn't your own. Instead, you are "one flesh" with your spouse! Married sex is the best sex.

Although society, which has been swindled by Satan, paints a different picture on who sex is for, and how it ought to be done, we must still obey all that God has to say about sex. If we don't, we will not inherit the kingdom of God, as mentioned by the Apostle Paul in 1 Corinthians 6:9-10 (NIV).

Married sex is the best sex.

"Do you not know that wrongdoers will not inherit the kingdom of God? Do not be deceived: Neither the sexually immoral nor idolaters nor adulterers nor men who have sex with men nor thieves nor the greedy nor drunkards nor slanderers nor swindlers will inherit the kingdom of God."

Christian Sex Ed. Fact

Did you know that if a husband accused his wife of not being a virgin after consummating the marriage through sex, there would be a mini-trial?

First, the parents of the bride brought the elders of town together to prove she was a virgin. They then took the sheets used during sexual intercourse and displayed them in front of the elders of the town. If the sheet had blood on it, the husband had to pay a fine for giving the wife a bad name. He also could not divorce her.

But if no blood was found on the sheets, the Bible says, *She shall be brought to the door of her father's house, and there the men of her town shall stone her to death* (Deuteronomy 22:21, NIV). This story shows that a woman's virginity was sacred in the Old Testament. It was only meant to be shared with her husband.

POP QUIZ

Yes, I'm the teacher who gives homework on the first day!

CHAPTER 101 QUIZ

1. From the Millennial Generation to Generation Z, how much has the average age of virginity loss dropped?

A. 1.11
B. 1.07
C. 0.97
D. 0.93

2. Who was the second couple mentioned in the Bible to have sex?

A. Abel and his wife
B. Solomon and his wife
C. Cain and his wife
D. Seth and his wife

3. In what chapter of Genesis does sex happen for the first time?

A. Genesis 2
B. Genesis 4
C. Genesis 3
D. Genesis 1

4. (At least) how many Scriptures are there in the New Testament that forbid sex outside of marriage?

5. In the Old Testament, a woman would get stoned if she got married and her husband found out she wasn't a virgin.

True or False

CHAPTER 101 QUIZ ANSWERS

1. From the Millennial Generation to Generation Z, how much has the average age of virginity loss dropped?

A. 1.11
B. 1.07
C. 0.97
D. 0.93

Answer: A – 1.11 years

2. Who was the second couple mentioned in the Bible to have sex?

A. Abel and his wife.
B. Solomon and his wife.
C. Cain and his wife.
D. Seth and his wife.

Answer: C – Cain and his wife.

3. In what chapter of Genesis does sex happen for the first time?

A. Genesis 2
B. Genesis 4
C. Genesis 3
D. Genesis 1

Answer: B – Genesis 4.

4. (At least) how many Scriptures are there in the New Testament that forbid sex outside of marriage?

Answer: At least twenty Scriptures.

5. In the Old Testament, a woman would get stoned if she got married and her husband found out she wasn't virgin.

True or False

Answer: **TRUE** – A woman was expected to remain a virgin until marriage, and it was shameful for her to have premarital sex while still living in her father's house.
(See Deuteronomy 22 for more information).

NOTE: Throughout this book, the terms "sinful lust" and "lust" are used interchangeably. To better understand the author's definition of "lust," review the definition in the glossary at the back of the book.

102

SEXUAL ADDICTI🧠N

It was my freshman year of college and the first week of Psychology 105, Introduction to Psychology. The class was packed with over 800 students. I had never seen so many students in one class. To ensure that we were all paying attention, the teacher gave us the first rule: "No website browsing allowed in class." To prevent this from happening, our professor had undercover teaching assistants spread throughout the class to watch us. These assistants would often peek over our shoulders at our laptops to make sure we weren't looking at anything but Psychology 105 work.

One particular day after class, as we were all exiting the room, we heard our professor yell loudly at a student, "Leave! Get out!"

The student replied, almost begging, "No! I'm sorry. Please! I won't do it again."

Finally, our professor said, "I already told you that you can't watch porn during class! Get out!" Turns out that one of the teaching assistants caught my classmate watching porn on his laptop during class more than once. For that reason, he got kicked out. As he made his way to the door, everyone stood around in shock, as if to say, "What just happened?"

The most surprising part to us all was that he was so infatuated with sex that he had to watch porn in a setting of more than 800 students. What made matters even worse was that class was only fifty minutes long. He couldn't wait, though. This led me to wonder, *Could sex (and/or sexual behaviors) really be that addictive?*

After all, prison cells are full of serial rapists, who are serving life sentences simply because they couldn't control their sexual urges. Men and women are getting divorced every day because of adultery. Then there's another population of people who watch porn and masturbate for hours every day.

What is it about sex that leads people to forget that their compulsive sexual behaviors come with great consequences? That question made me want to dig deeper and look at sex from a completely different angle. That is *the science behind sexual addiction*. Let's start by first addressing what sexual addiction is.

Sexual Addiction:

Sexual addiction is when a person loses control over their sexual desires and has become dependent on excessive amounts of sexual activity, in spite of the negative outcomes that follow. Furthermore, you know it's an addiction when the individual must engage in high amounts of sexual activity to flee from the feelings of *withdrawal*, which is the first symptom of addiction.

SYMPTOM #1: Experiencing withdrawals when not engaging in sexual behavior.

OVERVIEW

Withdrawals happen when your body becomes dependent on sex (or sexual behaviors) and you go for a long period of time without fulfilling that desire. These withdrawals can start by sending sexual signals to your body through extreme horniness, letting you know that your body is ready for its sexual dose.

If your body doesn't respond fast enough to these signals, you may experience extreme agitation, sexual cravings, loss of focus, inability to sleep and/or anxiety— which are all signs of withdrawal. Furthermore, these symptoms will intensify tremendously if something stimulates you sexually and you don't respond with sexual pleasure.

I hurried to the bathroom and masturbated.

I know that part of the symptom far too well. There was a moment in middle school when I saw a girl's thong underwear. After being instantly turned on by what I saw, I needed sexual gratification immediately! It was so bad that I couldn't focus in class. I needed an immediate orgasm. So, I asked my teacher if I could be excused to go to the bathroom. I hurried to the bathroom and masturbated. After masturbating, my focus came back.

In those moments, it was like a light switch got turned on in me. The only way to turn it off was by pleasing myself sexually. If that switch didn't get turned off, I wasn't able to focus on anything else.

Sadly, loss of focus is just one of the many withdrawals that an addict will experience. If the addict doesn't seek help, these withdrawals will severely interfere with their daily life.

SYMPTOM #2: Your desires for sex interfere with your daily life.

OVERVIEW

An example of this symptom would be a woman who is regularly late to work because she stays up late at night, watching pornography. In more severe instances, the woman will even miss work entirely so that she can spend the day indulging in her sexual fantasies.

People who display these symptoms don't tend to have time for anyone or anything else. It's not that they don't want to go places. Their addictive behaviors have just driven them to a place of isolation. They remain isolated because they can't stop giving their body what it's craving. Some are even afraid of being in a setting, like school or work, because they know they will be unable to give in on the spot to their body's desires.

Sadly, many who battle with sexual addiction live this life of interruption and isolation. Many have tried to break this addiction in hopes of having a normal life. However, they have been unable to do so, which leads us to symptom #3.

SYMPTOM #3: Unable to reduce time spent engaging in sexual behaviors.

OVERVIEW

People suffering from this symptom are entirely aware of the harmful effects their behaviors may cause. Because of that, they often make promises to themselves, such as:

"I'm done masturbating!"

"No more porn for the rest of the week!"

"This is the last time I'm having sex with a prostitute!"

Many people make these promises with good intentions and high hopes of ending their sexual behaviors. Unfortunately, no matter how many promises they make, or how many different techniques they try, they still fall short. After many failed attempts, feelings of shame and guilt come in because their addictive behaviors don't stop.

Concurrently to these excessive sexual behaviors, other areas in the body are impacted, such as the dopamine in the brain — which leads us to one of the critical contributors behind sex addiction.

Two Contributors to Sex Addiction

1. Excessive Sex, Dopamine Overload and Depletion

A key component within the brain that can lead to sex addiction is dopamine. Dopamine is a neurotransmitter that gets released when someone does something pleasurable. In this case, when someone has sex, or engages in sexual activity, dopamine is released. This lets the brain know that the body enjoys this pleasure and wants more of it because it's rewarding.

When someone has sex, or engages in sexual activity, dopamine is released.

This process becomes dangerous when an individual has excessive amounts of sexual activity because excessive amounts of dopamine are released. This leads to the depletion of their dopamine receptors (exhaustion). The body only has so much dopamine that it can release in a certain span of time.

Another way to put it is like this: the chemical in the brain (dopamine) that is responsible for communicating pleasure, giving a sexual high, and yielding the rewarding feeling of sex—is emptied. As a result of this emptying, the individual doesn't experience the same rewarding feeling or sexual high while having sex as they did before, which then leads to them experiencing sexual withdrawals.

To run away from the feelings of withdrawal, the individual will engage in even more sex, hoping to get the same reward as they did before the depletion. It is during this process that addiction is formed because the individual seeks to run away from the symptoms of withdrawal by engaging in more sexual activity.

I'll use myself as an example. When I was younger, I used to masturbate to pornography for several hours a day (*excessive amounts of dopamine being released*). Over time, my brain grew tolerant to these sexual behaviors and I didn't get the same enjoyment that I used to get (*dopamine depletion*). Therefore, to get the enjoyment that I used to have before *dopamine's depletion*, I had to watch more porn videos and masturbate longer (*running away from withdrawals)*, which formed addiction—an addiction that was a result of my excessive sexual behaviors.

2. Victim of Sexual Assault at an Early Age

Sexual addiction can also stem from someone being a victim of sexual assault at a young age. Moreover, it's dangerous for a child to experience sexual arousal because it awakens an underdeveloped part of the nervous system. This early awakening leads to the child believing that sexual feelings are normal and needed. Those feelings then lead to sexual dependency at a young age, which can later turn into sexual addiction.

However, to prove that childhood sexual abuse can lead to the victim having heightened interests in sex at an early age, I surveyed 250 people. I asked the question, "Did being sexually assaulted as a child push you toward a sexual interest or away from a sexual interest?"

In the results, 74% (186 people) said being sexually assaulted as a child pushed them toward an interest in sex. On the contrary, 26% (64 people) said that being sexually assaulted as a child pushed them away from an interest in sex.

The above survey statistics reveal to us that, if you're a child victim of sexual assault, you're more likely to be interested in and engage in sexual behaviors at an early age. This, in turn, makes it more possible for sexual addiction to form.

I became even more convinced of this after reading through nearly a hundred comments on my social media page. Many who were sexually assaulted said it gave them unnatural sexual desires, pornography addictions and masturbation addictions.

Nevertheless, whether being sexually assaulted as a child led to one's addiction, or excessive amounts of sex did, there are treatments available. These treatments are designed to help heal you, guide you into better decision making, remove you from your sexual addictive behaviors and control your sexual impulses.

Treatment Options

THERAPY

Cognitive Behavioral Therapy (CBT)
A common psychotherapy that is used to treat someone struggling with sexual addiction. The goal of this type of therapy is to help individuals find out what is triggering their sexual behaviors. Furthermore, it helps individuals stop engaging in compulsive sexual behaviors by finding healthy outlets.

Couples Therapy
Many who struggle with sexual addiction are too ashamed, or too afraid, of letting their partner know that they have such struggles. Therefore, they live their life full of secrets with transgressions of adultery, porn and masturbation—all behind their partner's back. As you can imagine, the effects of those addictive behaviors can weigh heavily on a relationship. This is where couples therapy comes in. It is a place for the two to communicate with full transparency, bring understanding to the situation, and bring healing from the pain that the addiction has caused to both individuals—the afflicted and the afflicter.

Group Therapy (Sex Addicts Anonymous)
The goal of group therapy is to help individuals overcome sexual addiction and maintain sexual sobriety. Some people in this form of therapy will practice abstinence, while some simply need to end their compulsive sexual behaviors. These goals are achieved through step-by-step guides that help ensure sexual sobriety. Group therapy also serves as a place to talk about your sexual addiction struggles in a judgment-free zone. This is key because most who struggle with sexual addiction never talk about it due to fear of judgment and shame. Without talking about it, they never receive the tips and help needed to overcome their addiction. But, in this type of therapy, you can find a place of hope, healing, help and encouragement. You will also meet with people who have the same struggles as you.

Medicine

Naltrexone
Along with therapy, medicine can play a key role in overcoming sexual addiction. One medication used to do so is Naltrexone. Interestingly, its original purpose was to treat alcoholics. But it's now also used to medicate sex addicts because it helps reduce the high of sex by controlling the amount of dopamine released. With a lessened high for sex, the desires for excessive amounts of it, and desires for masturbation, will drop. This makes it easier for the individual to stop and achieve homeostasis.

NOTE: Naltrexone doesn't remove the symptoms of withdrawal that accompany not having sex.

Antidepressants
Health professionals recommend the use of antidepressants for those battling sexual addiction. The side effects of antidepressants include having a lower interest in sex, difficulties in becoming aroused, and not enjoying sex as much as before. Ultimately, the chemicals in antidepressants lower a person's libido (sex drive). With a lowered libido, the addict will engage in less sexually addictive behaviors.

Class Wrap-Up

As seen throughout today's lesson, sex addiction can have serious implications. If you happen to be struggling with any of the symptoms, please seek help. There are plenty of resources, forms of therapy and support groups to help you overcome sexual addiction. Pursue the help you need so you can start enjoying your life to the fullest!

Seven Quick Signs That You May Be Struggling With Sexual Addiction

1. You engage in frequent one-night stands.
2. Your sexual behaviors have ruined your life.
3. You'll do anything to get sexual gratification.
4. You habitually watch pornography and masturbate.
5. Your desire for sex often interrupts your daily activities.
6. Your sexual behaviors and urges have become uncontrollable.
7. You experience withdrawals when not engaging in sexual behaviors.

103
XXX

held my breath as my parents signed onto the computer after I had just finished watching porn. Anxiously, I waited to hear, "Dane, what is this? Come here!" The thought of hearing those words killed me. So immediately, I began to think of these lies I could use, just in case I got caught:

"My friend told me to go to that website!"
"I don't know how that got there."
"It wasn't me."

> **PORNOGRAPHY**
> Sexual explicit magazines, photographs, and videos with the intent to arouse one sexually. These pornographic items often include nudity, acts of sex, group orgies, and other erotic behaviors.

Thankfully, I didn't have to use those lies that day. As my parents signed off the computer and went into their room, I blew a sigh of relief, and said, "Thank you, Jesus!"

While I enjoyed watching porn when I was growing up, it came with one big struggle: *not getting caught.* After all, our household usually had one computer and the entire family shared it. This meant that I had to cover up all of my tracks after watching porn. I deleted the browser history, cleared the cookies and the cache, and cleared the address bar. I also couldn't forget to clear the Google search bar. I'm convinced that many people got caught watching porn because of that good ole' Google search bar.

Nevertheless, some computers made it easy to delete the search history. I had the option to use the "delete all search history" button. The only problem was that it looked suspicious the next time someone had to use the computer.

To prevent suspicions, I'd type in a few non-pornographic sites in the search engine to make it look like that was my browsing history. That, at times, didn't work though because pornography always made the computer run slower. Therefore, you'd have to run clean sweeps of the computer often just to get things to run smoothly again.

That's how I grew up watching porn in the mid-2000s. What's interesting though is that how I watched it growing up was entirely different than how it was viewed in its origin.

The Evolution of Pornography

Thousands of years ago when people got turned on, they didn't have *Playboy Magazine* or *Pornhub*. Instead, they had to walk into caves and look at the carved images of men and women having sex on cave walls. Since caves didn't have any lights, people had to carry torches inside the caves to view their favorite sexual carvings.

Along with cave porn, the only other alternative for watching porn came through viewing erected statues of people engaging in sexual acts. These statues were composed of clay, wood, bones or stone. To this day, many of them are still standing and have become favorite tourist destinations throughout our world.

Fast-forward past these pornographic structures to the 1700s, where we saw the next major shift for pornography appearing through literature by way of erotica novels. One novel in particular that stamped its mark in the history of pornographic literature was *Memoirs of a Woman of Pleasure (Fanny Hill)* by John Cleland. In great detail, this book follows the sex life of a young female prostitute in London. Due to its pornographic nature, the book was banned, and author John Cleland was jailed in London. He was soon released, but the book was still banned, leaving people no choice but to pirate this steamy book. It wasn't until over two hundred years later that the ban was lifted, and *Memoirs of a Woman of Pleasure* was then allowed to legally be published in the U.S. and, a little later, in the U.K., where it originated.

Nevertheless, though pornography in literature faced these

types of persecutions, pornography as a whole didn't stop. It continued to emerge as technology developed. There was one technological advancement that enabled pornography to skyrocket: the invention of the camera in the early 1800s. Not long after the camera's invention, women started posing nude for photographs, which allowed people to carry pornographic photos at all times.

As time progressed, these photographs were made in sequence and, in 1878, the first black and white films were made. Now, pornography had another gateway. Not too many years later, the first pornographic films were produced.

About half a century later, Hugh Hefner came on the scene and took pornography to another level. Hugh Hefner was the creator of one of the world's top men's magazines of all-time: *Playboy*.

Playboy featured images of nude women and, at times, sold millions of copies a month. This became a new, hefty way for people to indulge in their love for pornography. All a person had to do was subscribe to *Playboy* and they would receive magazines filled with women posing nude, which made porn even more accessible.

Accessibility was the key component to growth in the industry of pornography. The more accessible it was, the more people had the chance to buy it, which meant more revenue for the industry. One invention in particular brought in loads of revenue and made it more accessible than ever before. That was the Internet, which came on the scene in the 1980s.

It was through the Internet that porn users were no longer limited to viewing the same pornographic photos and videos. Now, they had the option to watch whatever genre they wanted, whenever they wanted, by desktop computer, laptop, cell phone, tablet, gaming console and even virtual reality.

With this type of accessibility, people started spending thousands of dollars a month on pornography. With majority thanks to the Internet, pornography has become a multi-billion-dollar industry and is a leading economic sector in U.S. entertainment.

As you can tell, many people love pornography. But just what is it exactly about porn that has so many people watching it? After much research and self-reflection, I've pinpointed five major reasons why people watch porn.

Why Do People Watch Pornography?

1. Vicarious Living

The first reason why people watch porn is because it is a form of vicarious living. Porn allows people to live out their sexual fantasies through their imagination. For example, a male who loves brunette women can watch a porn video of a brunette having sex and live vicariously through the man she's having sex with. In other words, people can put themselves in the position that the man is in and enjoy the scene from the comfort of their own home.

When I was in middle school, I had a huge crush on this girl. I wanted to know what it'd be like to encounter her sexually. Then, one day, I stumbled across a pornographic video. The woman in the video looked just like the girl I had a crush on. I was hooked on this video because, through masturbation, it made me feel like I was having sex with her. The girl didn't like me back, but I felt like I had a piece of her through that video.

85% of Christians have struggled with pornography.
[1100 respondents]
(Survey via @ChristianSexEd Instagram)

2. It's an Escape

For some, pornography isn't entirely about pleasure. It's an escape from their ailing issues. Whether it is stress, low self-esteem, loneliness, anxiety, obsessive thoughts or depression, porn takes the edge off what they're going through. Porn is their friend who lightens their heavy loads. It takes them to a place where their problems don't exist.

3. Horniness

Porn is a fast and easy way to satisfy sexual cravings. Moreover, if an individual is horny, and can't get sex because they have no one to call or can't afford it, they can watch it for free on the Internet and masturbate.

4. To Learn About Sex

Many people use pornography as a teacher. People who are inexperienced in the bedroom will watch it to learn about sex. Although porn is staged, it shows the viewer many different sexual positions. Although I don't recommend it at all, some married men and women also find porn as a helpful way to learn new tricks and to keep things spicy in the bedroom.

5. Arousal Before Sex

In many cases, before sex, men have a hard time getting erected and women have a hard time lubricating (getting wet). If you've ever been in that position before, you know that it's extremely embarrassing. Not only is it embarrassing, but it can also make the person that you're getting ready to have sex with feel like they are unattractive or not good in the bedroom. To solve that problem, a lot of people watch porn prior to sex, so that they don't have any issues getting aroused.

The Effects of Pornography

With the understanding of why people watch porn, it's essential that we dive into the effects of porn. Often, porn is viewed simply as innocent fun; however, there are lasting effects that pornography can have on your life.

1. Breeds Perversion

Whenever I watched porn from the leading websites, I came across videos titled, "Father having sex with stepdaughter while mom is not home." In these videos, the stepdaughters looked like they were fourteen years old, if not younger.

It never hit me until recently that those videos are perverted. They give birth to perverted thoughts and behaviors. After all, why would anyone want to sleep with his or her stepchild? And why did porn place such an emphasis on grown women looking underage?

I believe it's because the demonic spirit behind porn is trying to channel something into people that shouldn't be there. That is a lust for underage girls (pedophilia). If you watch videos like that long enough, you become desensitized to the underage incest that's being promoted. You also open yourself up to receive that lust. You can only take in so much foul material before it leaks into other areas of your life. Therefore, it's these types of perverted actions in the porn industry that cause porn users to become incestuous child abusers.

However, it doesn't stop there. Porn becomes even more perverted. One of the most perverted things that I ever stumbled across while watching porn was a woman having sex with a horse. When I first saw this, I was shocked! Why on earth would anyone want to have sex with an animal?

I bet those porn stars never imagined that they would have sex with animals.

And I bet the people who watch that type of porn never imagined masturbating to humans having sex with animals. Nonetheless, when you go deep-sea fishing in lust, your net will bring up more than you imagined. Therefore, don't dabble in porn. You don't know how far it'll take you or what door of perversion you'll walk into because of it.

2. Gives Birth to Abusive Sex Practices

Porn that involves verbal or physical abuse gets the most views. It also brings in the most revenue annually. The more violent the porn scene, the more money it makes. The average consumer doesn't care for romantic porn. They'd rather watch someone get choked, spit on, tied up or verbally abused during the sexual acts.

Porn is fake and gives birth to unrealistic expectations.

From a consumer's standpoint, these videos are dangerous. The more of them you watch and take in, the more it shows up in your own sex life. Many porn addicts transfer these abusive practices into the bedroom in attempt to live out what they've seen on the screen.

Unfortunately, what many don't know is that pornography is fake. It's staged.

It's abuse masked with smiles and orgies. Behind the scenes, women are crying and breaking down as they're encouraged or forced to finish these abusive scenes for the film. If you like these abusive scenes, don't be surprised when you feel the need to reenact them and end up developing abusive tendencies of your own.

3. Breaks Marital Intimacy and Leads to Divorce

There is one thing you will never see in porn: genuine affection. Porn only has one goal: to arouse the consumer. It completes that by focusing solely on pleasure, which leads to a distorted view of sex. This causes a person to view their spouse as an object of pleasure. This is why many porn addicts have a hard time connecting intimately during sex with their spouse because pornography didn't show them intimacy. It only showed them orgies.

Maybe you've even heard of stories where a wife says this to her husband during sex: "I want you to take your time and love me. It just feels like you want to *do* me." These are the behaviors that porn gives birth to—behaviors that seek pleasure over connection.

While sex is purposed for marital pleasure, sex doesn't stop there. It's supposed to be intimate, passionate and affectionate. The key ingredient that makes sex beautiful is love! There's nothing better than making love to your spouse. Pornography robs you of that gift by making it hard to connect intimately with your spouse. This is because porn gives you the option to explore your sexual fantasies through one of its hundreds of genres, including your choice of body type; breast size; nipple size; butt size; penis size; hair color; hair length; eye color; race; and even fetish.

Quite frankly, that's a long list for your spouse to keep up with. It's no wonder why intimacy breaks in the relationship. Nevertheless, to help bring the sexual connection back, many people close their eyes during sex and imagine that their spouse is their favorite porn star. That won't ever be good enough, though. They will always want the real thing. Eventually, this will lead the spouse who is addicted to porn to seek fulfillment of their sexual fantasies elsewhere.

It may start with them visiting live sex chat rooms. Then, it may gradually grow to private shows, personal inbox messages of sexual nature and sexting. Before you know it, they will be meeting up for sex with outsiders. While they may not have sex with their favorite porn star, they'll pursue the next best thing, because porn makes you bored with what you have and leads you to adultery. Thus, there is a positive connection between watching pornography and committing adultery.

To combat the above effects of pornography, below is a nine-step guide to help put an end to your porn habits.

Nine-Step Guide to Stop Watching Porn

STEP 1: DON'T LIVE IN DENIAL.

Do not be deceived. Porn is much more than "just a little struggle." It can be detrimental to your life. Freedom from pornography starts with admitting there is a problem, then making intentional behavior changes.

STEP 2: IDENTIFY

Many times, pornography is a symptom of a greater root problem. What problem(s) are you running away from that cause you to find solace in pornography? After you've identified that problem, work toward finding a solution. Once solved, you ideally eliminate a key contributor to your porn habits.

STEP 3: ACCOUNTABILITY.

Find a trusted *godly* individual who can keep you accountable and check in periodically along your journey to freedom. This person will be someone you can confide in and call in moments of weakness. This person will also be the one who has committed to pray for you in this area.

STEP 4: GO COLD TURKEY.

You cannot wean yourself off porn. You must cut it all off at once. Don't deceive yourself into thinking that you can watch porn in moderation and, eventually, you just won't have the desire to watch it. That's a lie from the enemy. The more you watch porn—even in moderation—the deeper the pit you dig yourself into. Therefore, you must go cold turkey and stop watching it. It won't be easy to do at first and, yes, you will have withdrawals. But it will be worth it.

STEP 5: BLOCK.

Whatever is luring you back into your porn addiction needs to be blocked. This may include blocking phone numbers, television shows, and certain social media pages. This may seem extreme, but it only takes the slightest temptation to open the door and lure you back to pornography. I can't tell you how many times I've crawled back to porn because of something I saw on social media that aroused me in the moment. After I was initially turned on, I had to see more. Porn was that open door. For that reason, block anything and everything that gets in your way of freedom.

STEP 6: DENY YOUR FLESH.

When tempted to go on your phone, laptop or tablet to watch porn, take ownership of the moment and deny your flesh. Initially, this will be challenging because you're not giving your body what it's craving and what it's used to receiving. However, the more you deny your flesh, the more your spiritual man grows. Then eventually, over time, it'll get easier to reject porn.

STEP 7: READ THE BIBLE, FAST AND PRAY.

It's through reading the Bible that you discover that watching pornography is a sin of sexual lust, which Jesus condemns in Matthew 5:28. Through *fasting*, you focus on God, deny your flesh and realign yourself with Him. Lastly, through *prayer*, you receive strength to break through the sinful habits of porn.

STEP 8: GET COUNSELING

If you're dealing with an addiction to pornography, see a counselor. Counseling will help you identify the cause of your addiction, then walk you through the process of coming out of it.

STEP 9: CELEBRATE VICTORY.

Note on your calendar the day of the last time you watched porn. This will be your "deliverance from pornography" anniversary. Even if you watched porn yesterday, still mark it. Every seven days that you stay free from porn, celebrate that victory with an added session of prayer, worship and reading the Bible. This step of celebration will make you more spiritually fit, create motivation, and encourage you to stay free from the temporary pleasures of pornography.

Class Wrap-Up

While pornography may bring a fleeting satisfaction to the eyes, the catastrophes that accompany it aren't worth it. Porn ruins your finances, relationships, marriage, social life and sex life. Above all, it pulls you away from God because it's a sin of sexual lust (Matthew 5:28; Job 31:1).

In a world where porn has become a multi-billion-dollar industry, it's essential that people know these catastrophes. It's our duty to make them aware. We can do so by preaching the message of #AntiPorn to every person of every nation. The more we preach it, the more we snatch people out of hell and addiction. The more we preach it, the more deliverance sweeps through our homes, communities, churches, country and the world.

10 Quotes on Porn

1. Porn is addictive.
2. Porn breeds perversion.
3. Porn can lead to erectile dysfunction in men.
4. Porn destroys your sex life.
5. Porn takes the intimacy out of sex.
6. Porn makes you ungrateful for what your spouse has to offer in the bedroom.
7. Porn leads to adultery.
8. Porn is fake and gives birth to unrealistic expectations.
9. Porn brings pleasure to the eyes, but danger to the soul.
10. When you eliminate porn from your marriage, you'll be able to enjoy your spouse to the fullest.

A NIGHT WITH THE KING

Twenty-first century television has nothing on the sex scandals that took place in the Bible! Growing up, however, I thought the Bible was boring—that was until I read about the great men of God who couldn't keep their pants up, like me! What I love most about the Bible is that God doesn't hold back, nor sugarcoat, their sexual transgressions. He goes into great detail. I believe that God reveals so much of their shortcomings so that we know what *not* to do. For that reason, we will use this chapter as an opportunity to look deeply into the night with the king, as well as explore the lives of other biblical characters who fell into lust.

King David

The overlooked, smelly shepherd boy, David, was in charge of tending to the sheep. He also was the one who slayed Goliath and cut off his head. He was Saul's armor bearer and a man after God's own heart. He killed tens of thousands of people in war and eventually became Israel's second king. He was a man of God who started from the bottom, found his way to the top, but almost lost it all because of one decision.

King David's army was at war. He was supposed to be leading his troops in battle. But, instead, he decided to stay at home. While at home that evening, David got up from his bed and went to the roof of his palace. There, he saw a woman named Bathsheba bathing. Her extreme beauty immediately struck him. He couldn't help but stare at her nude body glistening in the moonlight as she washed herself. David was so intrigued by this woman that he had to find out more about her. Looking at her from afar was not enough. Upon inquiring of her, David found out that she was the husband of Uriah, a man in his army. Even though she was married, David didn't care. Consumed with lust, he sent his servants on a short journey to bring Bathsheba up to his palace. The Bible doesn't tell us much about what takes place when Bathsheba enters the palace.

Nonetheless, I can imagine that as she entered, King David offered her a tour.

I bet he started off with his lovely dining area, then maybe showed her his prized possessions. Perhaps he showed her the slingshot that he used

He couldn't help but stare at her nude body glistening in the moonlight as she washed herself.

to slay Goliath. Finally, near the conclusion of the tour, I imagine that he led Bathsheba up his palace stairs. I can picture their hands both sliding up the rails before finally entering his room. As Bathsheba entered, I imagine that she said something like, "What a lovely place you have, David. What an even more lovely view!"

David, who was probably grinning, walked up behind her, wrapped his arms around her waist, and said, "Yes, and you're the best part of that view."

From that moment, it was a wrap. This is where the Bible tells us that David did the unthinkable. He had sex with a married man's wife.

Following that passionate night of sex, I don't imagine that David expected anything further from Bathsheba. After all, she was married. This leads me to believe that David didn't expect anything more than a one-night stand. Yet, not too long after they had sex, Bathsheba sent word to David that she is pregnant. This alarmed David. So, he did what many have done before: he tried to cover up his sin so that he could avoid the consequences.

David didn't expect anything more than a one-night stand.

In doing so, David called Uriah home from war, sent a gift to his house, and told him to go home and get clean. David's goal was for Uriah to sleep with Bathsheba so that it would appear as if the child was Uriah's—not David's. But Uriah didn't go home. The next day, David asked Uriah why he didn't go home after his military campaign.

Uriah, being an honorable man, said, *"The ark and Israel and Judah are staying in tents, and my commander Joab and my lord's men are camped in the open country. How could I go to my house to eat and drink and make love to my wife? As surely as you live, I will not do such a thing* (2 Samuel 11:11, NIV)!

Consequently, David was then faced with another dilemma because Uriah would not go home and sleep with his wife. So, David made one last desperate attempt to cover his tracks and protect his reputation. In doing so, he invited Uriah to his house and got him drunk, hoping that Uriah would go home and have drunken sex with Bathsheba.

But again, David woke up to find out that Uriah didn't go home. At this point, David felt like he had no other choice but to take Uriah out. David sent Uriah back to war, with a letter for Joab stating, *"Put Uriah out in front where the fighting is fiercest. Then withdraw from him so he will be struck down and die"* (2 Samuel 11:15, NIV).

Just as it was written, so it happened. Uriah carried his letter of death and, upon returning to war, he was killed in battle, along with others, because of David's decision. Preceding Uriah's death, Bathsheba was notified and mourned for Uriah. However, once the period of mourning ended, she married King David, and gave birth to their child, a son.

Consequences of Sin

With Uriah dead and out of the picture, King David probably believed that he had escaped the consequences of sin. After all, he committed adultery and murder, and had now married another man's wife. However, Proverbs 15:3 (NIV) reminds us, *The eyes of the LORD are everywhere, keeping watch on the wicked and the good.* This was a wicked moment for David, and the Lord wouldn't allow him to escape the consequences of sin. Therefore, God sent

Nathan, a prophet, to confront David about his transgressions. Part of the word of the Lord to David from the prophet Nathan was:

"This is what the Lord says: 'Out of your own household I am going to bring calamity on you. Before your very eyes I will take your wives and give them to one who is close to you, and he will sleep with your wives in broad daylight. You did it in secret, but I will do this thing in broad daylight before all Israel'" (2 Samuel 12:11-12, NIV).

After this prophetic word was spoken, David acknowledged his sin and repented. God forgave him and spared his life. Though David's life had been spared, his son, who was conceived through adultery with Bathsheba, was going to die as judgment. Then, just as the prophet Nathan prophesied, *"Out of your own household, I am going to make calamity on you"* (2 Samuel 12:11, NIV). So, calamity came upon David from his own household. Some of this calamity included his sons, Absalom and Adonijah, attempting to take over his throne. Then, Absalom had sex with David's concubines, and his son, Amnon, raped his daughter, Tamar.

As we can see, David's sinful actions not only affected him, but his seeds, as well. This leads me to wonder if David ever took time to think about the consequences that could come with adultery and murder. Every sinful thing that David did could've been avoided if he'd only considered a few things before he committed sin.

Think Before You Act

One of the first things that David should've carefully considered was his decision to stay home from war. As the God-ordained king of Israel, he was responsible for leading his army to victory, which required him to be at war with his troops. However, instead of going on the military campaign, David decided to stay home.

In the Word, 2 Samuel 11:1 (NIV) says, *In the spring, at the time when kings go off to war, David sent Joab out with the king's men and the whole Israelite army. They destroyed the Ammonites and besieged Rabbah. But David remained in Jerusalem.*

We may not know why David decided to stay home, but we do know that his decision to do so resulted in him committing sin. Had

David just went on the military campaign, like he was anointed to do, he never would've seen Bathsheba bathing. If he never saw Bathsheba bathing, he never would've been in a position to commit those atrocious sins. Through those atrocious sins, David shows us that leaving your God-ordained post will set you up for failure. Hence, we must stay focused on the assignment that God has called us to so that we don't fall victim to sexual sin, like David.

Secondly, David had a decision to make while he was on the roof, gazing at Bathsheba. He could have either continued to lust after her naked body or turned his head and went back to bed. Sadly, David didn't choose the latter. He drooled over her body and inquired about her. Through his inquiry, he found out that she was married, which was another opportunity for him to choose to do the right thing. David knew that it was wrong to pursue Bathsheba because adultery was forbidden in the Mosaic law and Ten Commandments. Nevertheless, David still summoned Bathsheba to his palace for a night with the king.

Also, one of the most interesting things about this story, which I believe David failed to take into consideration, was that Bathsheba was fertile. David knew she was fertile because she just received purification from her monthly uncleanness (2 Samuel 11:4). For a woman to be purified from her monthly uncleanness, she had to wait seven days after her menstrual cycle ended, which was a requirement under the Mosaic law (Leviticus 15:19, 28).

Furthermore, under Jewish customs, a woman was to take a Mikvah (ritual bath) after the seven days, which was for purification. But due to the regulations regarding Mikvahs, not every woman had their own place for this type of bath, especially if she was poor. We know that Bathsheba was poor because, in the prophet Nathan's prophecy in 2 Samuel 12:3 (NIV), her husband, Uriah, was called a "poor man." He "had nothing except one little ewe lamb he bought." That "little ewe lamb" was Bathsheba. Because she was poor, it's likely that her Mikvah was done in one of the assigned areas throughout the community.

So, it's possible that while David was on his roof, he saw Bathsheba bathing below in a Mikvah designated area. With David being a Jew and having multiple Jewish wives, he should have been familiar with the Jewish custom of Mikvahs because his wives followed them, as well.

David would've known that, at the time of these baths, women began fertility because their menstrual cycle just ended, which was when they became purified, and took these baths. So, *if* David knew Bathsheba was fertile while taking her Mikvah, why did he have sex with her? A wise man would've known better than to commit adultery with a fertile woman. The chances are too high that she could get pregnant. However, I don't believe David took this into consideration. He allowed lust to guide his decision, which resulted in him leaving his seed in her. It's through the seed that he left in Bathsheba that we are left with valuable lessons from his life.

Lessons from David

The first lesson that David teaches us is that lust will turn you into someone that you're not. Prior to King David falling into sexual sin, the Bible calls him "a man after God owns heart" (1 Samuel 13:14, NIV). Yet, after he fell into sexual sin, we saw a David we'd never seen before. We saw a David who completely lost his regard for the Lord.

We know this because it took David over nine months (through the course of Bathsheba's pregnancy) to repent of his sinful actions. How does it take a man after God's own heart over nine months to realize that he was wrong? What's even worse is that David may have never even repented of his sins had God not sent the prophet Nathan to rebuke him. That right there shows us the effects of lust and how it turned David from a man of God to a murderer, adulterer, and deceiver!

The second lesson that David teaches us happens to remind me of a huge waterpark that my family and I went to when I was younger. At this waterpark, there was an enormous slide that everyone desired to go down. In order to get to this slide, you had to wait behind a hundred people or more, while walking slowly up ten flights of wooden stairs. Although this wait in line was dreadful, we still walked up those wooden stairs with our feet burning because we wanted to experience the ride.

It took almost an hour to get to the front of the line, but it only took ten seconds to come down the slide. In David's case, it took him approximately twenty years to become the king of Israel after he had been anointed for the position. Yet, it only took him a few minutes to fall into sexual sin and almost lose it all.

What makes matters even worse is that many of those twenty years were spent going through hell. They were filled with persecution, death threats, attempted murders on his life, and running from Saul to finally become king. However, he almost lost it all because of one sexual sin.

That shows us that, no matter how high you climb, no matter how long it took, and no matter how hard it was to get to the top, the fall is still easy and fast. This leaves me with one question for David: Was that night with Bathsheba worth it?

David almost lost it all because of one sexual sin.

Other Bible Characters Who Fell Victim to Lust

THE INCESTUOUS SON, AMNON

Amnon was a man of lust, like his father, King David. However, his lust was different. It was incestuous. Amnon burned with love for his half-sister, Tamar. He loved her so much that it made him sick. She was a virgin and he knew that he couldn't be the one to break her hymen. But one day, he mustered up enough *perverted* courage to try. When Tamar refused him, he raped her. This wicked action led to his untimely murder.

If you don't get delivered, lust can turn you into a rapist or a pervert. It can even cause you to commit incest. Lust has no boundaries. Amnon grew up with his sister. He was supposed to be her protector. But instead, lust made her his victim.

SODOM AND GOMORRAH (GENESIS 19)

Sodom and Gomorrah were full of so much sin that God decided to destroy the entire land by fire and brimstone. But just before God rained down judgment on these two cities, He sent two angels to escort Lot and his family out of Sodom. After the angels arrived at Lot's house, the old and young men of the city surrounded Lot's house, seeking to have sex with the two men (angels). The townspeople of Sodom were so wicked that the very second someone new arrived into their town, they engaged them for an orgy. Such behavior lets us know that everybody in Sodom must've already had sexual relations with each other and engaged in innumerable orgies. That type of wickedness wouldn't go unpunished. This left God with no other choice, but to give them a fair penalty for their sexually sinful ways.

This story of Sodom and Gomorrah falls right in line with Romans 1:27 (NIV), which says, *In the same way the men also abandoned natural relations with women and were inflamed with lust for one another. Men committed shameful acts with other men and received in themselves the due penalty for their error.*

ELI'S PRIEST SONS (1 SAMUEL 2)

Eli's two sons, Hophni and Phinehas, were priests. They were tasked with teaching the people about the decrees the Lord gave them through Moses. Yet, Eli's sons did evil and, *slept with the women who served at the entrance to the tent of meeting* (1 Samuel 2:22, NIV). Interestingly, the same law they taught from, which forbid women from having sex before marriage, and purposed sex for only the husband and wife (Deuteronomy 22:21), was the same law that they caused the women who were serving to break.

Class Wrap-Up

As we saw throughout today's lesson, many people in the Bible fell short in sexual purity because they decided to follow lust, instead of God. Consequently, lust has only one ending point:

death (spiritual and/or physical). Nevertheless, each person who fell into lust had the chance to get right with God before it was too late. I can only imagine the number of warnings God gave them before finally raining down judgment and bringing their sins to the light. But even God bringing their sins to light can be counted as *mercy*. If God brings to light what someone did in the dark, it's because He's trying to bring them back into the light. Subsequently, God's end goal is to save a person's soul. He'll do whatever He can to lead them to repentance—even if it means exposing their sexual wickedness.

105
PROPHETIC WARNINGS

DREAMS AND VISIONS THAT GOD GAVE ME CONCERNING SEXUAL SIN

Since 2015, God has given me warnings about sexual sin and lust by visions and dreams. In this lesson of Christian Sex Ed., I will release some of the things that God has warned *me* about, as well as others.

2015: The Butler, The Pancakes and The Cat

It was a late night in my apartment, and I had just rolled over after having pre-marital sex. Immediately, God gave me a vision. In this vision, I was walking toward a butler who was holding a big stack of buttery pancakes. But, as I approached the pancakes, a cat jumped on top of them and ate them. The vision then repeated itself. In the vision this time, God showed me what everything meant.

First, the butler represented God. The pancakes were His blessings for me, and the cat was the devil. Every time the butler (God) held out my pancakes (blessings), the cat (the devil) would devour them because I was too busy fornicating. God was showing me that my lack of sexual purity was keeping me from reaching my blessings on time. Not only was my lack of purity causing a delay in me receiving my blessings, but it was also devouring them. The thought of missing out on God's blessings shook me. I could picture every good thing that God had in store for me slowly fading away, out of arm's reach.

If you want to experience the many blessings of God in your life, kick out all sexual sin. God is looking for a vacant room, one that is sexually sin-free, so that He can fill it up with His blessings. His blessings can't come in where sin has occupied space.

2018: Lust Has the Power to Break Through Any Ring

A PROPHETIC WARNING TO MARRIED INDIVIDUALS AND THOSE GETTING READY TO BE MARRIED

It was a typical night for me as I laid down for bed. However, to my surprise, God gave me an unexpected dream. This dream started with me randomly appearing in a nice hotel or penthouse lobby. I headed outside to the pools, and, to my surprise, I saw naked women everywhere. What made it even more shocking was that I could *smell* the lust and seduction in the air. In a sense, there was a heavy pollution of lust. I couldn't help but notice the stench of it.

With lust in the air, and women poolside, I wondered, *Am I married?* This question led me to look down at my wedding ring. To my complete shock, my white, silicon ring was broken. After seeing this, I immediately became worried. I asked myself, *Did I do something wrong? Did I commit adultery?* Amid these worries, this thought came to my mind: *The ring is silicon. It can easily break, and this breakage has nothing to do with adultery.* After this thought of denial, the dream ended.

> *I could smell the lust and seduction in the air.*

Right away, another dream started. Everything appeared to be the same as the first dream. I was in a lobby. I walked outside to the pool. I saw the women. But, this time, one small detail was different. Instead of my white silicon wedding ring, I was wearing my big, heavy golden ring that I had when I got married. Filled with dismay, I noticed this ring, too, was broken! At that moment, I couldn't deny what was breaking these rings. It was the surrounding women and lust. After coming to this realization, the dream ended, and I woke up.

When I first woke up, I was fearful and wondered, *Does this mean that I'm going to one day commit adultery, and my marriage will be over?* This thought pierced my mind because I have always wanted to remain adultery-free. Moreover, from the time of this dream until now, I hadn't been watching porn, masturbating, committing adultery or even flirting with women. To the glory of God, none of these things have happened in my marriage. I thank God for keeping my marriage pure. Nonetheless, God wanted to use me as His vessel to relay this dream and prophetic warning to everyone (including me). The message is clear: lust has the power to break through any ring.

It doesn't matter how long you've been married, how strong of a foundation you have, or how in love you and your spouse are. If you and your spouse don't rid yourself of lust, your marriage can, and will, be in jeopardy.

God proved that in this dream by using the big, heavy golden ring to represent years of love, strength and strong foundation. The white silicon ring represented less time, less strength and a weaker foundation. It didn't matter how strong the marriage was or was not. Lust was able to break through both rings (marriages).

This isn't anything new. Lust has destroyed many new marriages, as well as the ones with tens of years under their marital belt. Therefore, anyone battling with lust cannot live in denial (like the emotion God had me experience in the dream). One day, that lust will catch you slipping and destroy what God has put together.

Dream Disclaimer

I didn't want to reveal this dream because I didn't want it to appear that God was giving me a sexual dream. That wasn't the case. At no point during the dream was I tempted or enticed to sin. Instead, I was aware of the lustful surroundings. God used the nudity to reveal the severity of lust. In the Word, God has used nudity before to get His point across.

Below are three examples.

1. In Isaiah 20, God commanded the prophet Isaiah to walk around naked for three years as a sign of the troubles that

He would inflict on Egypt and Ethiopia. Although the Scripture says "naked," it's often debated as to whether or not Isaiah was completely naked with his genitalia exposed. Nonetheless, the Scripture still says he was "naked."

2. In 1 Samuel 19:23-24 (NIV), the spirit of God comes upon Saul. While prophesying, he took his clothes off and, *"lay naked all that day and all that night."*

3. Matthew 27:35 (NIV) says, *They divided up his clothes by casting lots.* When Jesus died for our sins, he was bloody, beaten and naked.

But even having knowledge of these things, I still wanted to make sure that God wanted me to release this dream. So, I asked Him. Within sixteen hours, God answered me. He gave me three out-of-the-blue confirmations that this dream had to be released.

November 9, 2018: Lust's Roller Coaster

The day before I was preparing to preach at a conference on purity, this wave of sleep hit me. Instantly, God took me into a dream. In this dream, I was riding a roller coaster with my hands in the air. I was having the time of my life. But, all of a sudden, as we got to the top of a steep drop, which was the best part of the ride, everything changed. I noticed that the roller coaster was coming to a sudden end, but not at the usual point. Instead, it was ending in dark, flaming fire. This roller coaster was going to the fire, and I couldn't jump out of because the lap (lust) bars had me completely strapped in.

Finally, as I was about to hit the fire, I immediately woke up out of the daze. This message came to me: "Lust is like a roller coaster, but with an unexpected end."

On the lust roller coaster, you'll have your hands up. You'll be careless, with no worries or fear—until one day, when you least expect it, that ride will end in fiery torment. You'll be so distracted by the pleasure that you won't even see the fire until it's too late.

Class Wrap-Up

These dreams and visions were pretty heavy, but they do serve a great purpose. They warn us of what could take place in our lives if we don't repent from sexual sin and lust. Therefore, we must all be completely right in God's sight, because the consequences of lust will last much longer than the time spent enjoying it.

MIDTERM

CHRISTIAN SEX ED. MIDTERM

1. When an individual engages in sexual activities, what is released?

A. Naltrexone
B. Libido and Naltrexone
C. Dopamine and Libido
D. Dopamine

2. From the Millennial Generation to Generation Z, how much has the average age of virginity loss dropped?

A. 1.11
B. 1.07
C. 0.97
D. 0.93

3. If you wanted to look at porn thousands of years ago, where would you do so?

4. What prophet in the Bible did God tell to walk around naked?

A. Elijah
B. Amos
C. Jeremiah
D. Isaiah

5. What percentage of Christians admitted to struggling with pornography at some point in their walk with God?

A. 62%
B. 81%
C. 61%
D. 85%

6. What medicine is used to cure sexual addiction?

A. H1N1
B. Naltrexone
C. Prilosec
D. Cialis

7. In what chapter of Genesis does sex happen for the first time?

A. Genesis 2
B. Genesis 4
C. Genesis 3
D. Genesis 1

8. What type of bath did a Jewish woman take after the completion of her menstrual cycle?

9. Who was the prophet who rebuked David on behalf of God?

A. Samuel
B. Elijah
C. Nathan
D. Jeremiah

10. Fill in the blank. "Lust has the power to break through any_____."

CHRISTIAN SEX ED. MIDTERM ANSWERS

1. When an individual engages in sexual activities, what is released?
A. Naltrexone
B. Libido and Naltrexone
C. Dopamine and Libido
D. Dopamine

Answer: D – Dopamine

2. From the Millennial Generation to Generation Z, how much has the average age of virginity loss dropped?
A. 1.11
B. 1.07
C. 0.97
D. 0.93

Answer: A – 1.11 years

3. If you wanted to look at porn thousands of years ago, where did you go?

Answer: Caves

4. What prophet in the Bible did God tell to walk around naked?
A. Elijah
B. Amos
C. Jeremiah
D. Isaiah

Answer: D – Isaiah

5. What percentage of Christians admitted to struggling with pornography at some point in their walk with God?

A. 62%
B. 81%
C. 61%
D. 85%

Answer: D – 85%

6. What medicine is used to cure sexual addiction?

A. H1N1
B. Naltrexone
C. Prilosec
D. Cialis

Answer: B – Naltrexone

7. In what chapter of Genesis does sex happen for the first time?

A. Genesis 2
B. Genesis 4
C. Genesis 3
D. Genesis 1

Answer: B – Genesis 4

8. What type of bath did a Jewish woman take after the completion of her menstrual cycle?

Answer: Mikvah

9. Who was the prophet who rebuked David on behalf of God?

A. Samuel
B. Elijah
C. Nathan
D. Jeremiah

Answer: C – Nathan

10. "Lust has the power to break through any_____."

Answer: ring

106
FORBIDDEN LINES

You're hanging with your boyfriend or girlfriend. All of a sudden, you feel something rise—your sexual hormones. With the mood just right, you debate whether or not to cross that forbidden line. You know it's a sin, but you can't resist. So, you give in and tell yourself:

We won't go too far.

We'll repent afterward.

This is the last time!

Five minutes later—you're doing the very thing you said you *wouldn't* do. And, after you finish doing it, your horniness is immediately replaced with conviction. You're now left repenting and promising God that you'll wait until marriage to cross that forbidden line again! That is, until the next week comes and you find yourself in the same position—breaking your promise to God once again.

I know this situation far too well. Sadly, so do many others. As a result of these impurities, the very relationships that God has put together have been crumbling into pieces. For that reason, in today's lesson of Christian Sex Ed., we will provide you with the proper tools to have a sexually pure relationship and not cross the forbidden lines. But, before doing that, it's imperative that we first discuss how far is "too far."

How Far Is Too Far?

For the most part, Christians accept the fact that pre-marital sex is a sin. It's too far, as we proved in Chapter 1. However, much controversy remains around the acts of foreplay that lead up to sex. Those acts include mutual masturbation, which is when a man fingers a woman or when a woman gives a man a hand job. It can also be when they perform these acts on themselves while the other person is present. Another act of foreplay is dry humping, which is when two people imitate the movements of sex on each other. This act can be done with or without clothes, but it doesn't involve any actual sexual penetration. Other acts of foreplay include kissing and licking the stomach, breasts, abs and other areas on the body. Lastly, a popular act of foreplay is oral sex, which is when a man or woman uses their mouth on the other person's genitals for sexual pleasure.

Many people question, "Is there enough biblical evidence to prove that these acts of foreplay are sinful for the unmarried?" I would say there is! Galatians 5:19 (KJV) says, *Now the works of the flesh are manifest, which are these; Adultery, fornication, uncleanness, lasciviousness.* If you read the next two verses, you'll see that these acts are forbidden. By engaging in them, you will not inherit the kingdom of God. Moreover, there is one specific word I want to emphasize in Galatians 5:19, which can be applicable to acts of foreplay: *lasciviousness.*

J.H. Thayer, a Bible scholar and an expert translator of the Greek (the original language of the New Testament Bible), defines lasciviousness as "wanton acts or manners as filthy words, indecent bodily movements, unchaste handling of males and females, etc."

"Unchaste handling of males and females" could be described as touching someone in a sexual manner, explicitly targeting the genital area. "Indecent bodily movements" can be described as moving your body in any sexual, lustful or lewd way. Under both of these translations of lasciviousness, the acts of mutual masturbation, dry humping, body kissing, and oral sex are sinful.

In addition to J.H. Thayer's definition, take another look at Galatians 5:19. Here, the Apostle Paul categorizes these different types of sexual sin. First, he calls out adultery, which is sexual intercourse outside of marriage by one or both parties. Second, he condemns fornication, which is sexual intercourse between two people that aren't married to each other or pre-marital sex. Third, he rebukes uncleanness, which can be defined as lustful impurities. Lastly, he mentions lasciviousness, which covers all other areas of sexual sin (e.g., foreplay, mutual masturbation, oral sex, dry humping, etc.). It's by no coincidence that he separates all four of these sins when dealing with sexual sin. I believe that he was covering all bases so that we would be crystal clear on the lines of sexual sin.

If the above Scripture, definitions, and answers don't convince you, though, one thing still makes acts of foreplay forbidden: sinful lust. Broadly defined, lust is: a very strong desire for someone or something, generally of a sexual nature. That definition doesn't completely capture the lust that the Bible condemns. (See Job 31:1; Proverbs 6:25; Matthew 5:28; Romans 1:26–27). The sinful lust that the Bible warns us against can be defined as the sexual coveting or objectification of someone that you're not married to. Additionally, sexual desires become sinful lust when they *willfully* manifest through the eyes, imaginations, thoughts, actions, and the heart with the intent to gain sexual gratification.

In other words, the only person that you can *willfully* think about or look at in a way that brings you *sexual gratification* is your spouse of the opposite sex. It's quite the challenge, if not impossible, to engage in foreplay without thinking about the person in a way that brings you sexual satisfaction. Therefore, we can conclude that sinful lust makes foreplay sin.

Now, with the overwhelming evidence that we have on what is too far sexually, let's look at some of the harmful effects of sexual impurity.

List of what's too far while unmarried:

1. Sex (review Chapter 1)
2. Mutual masturbation
3. Dry humping

4. Oral sex
5. All acts of foreplay
6. Kissing, hugging and touching (if sinful lust is involved)

NOTE: Sexual desires, attractions, and arousals aren't sin. Those are natural feelings that God has designed our bodies to have. However, if those feelings aren't stewarded by God's Word and if you obtain sexual satisfaction from them outside of marriage, it is sin.

The Effects of Sexual Impurity

CLOUDS YOUR JUDGMENT

Sex will always make you judge situations differently. Moreover, with lust clouding your judgment, it's easy to fall victim to good sex instead of good love. Meaning, you can be head over heels for someone solely because of the sexual intimacy you two share! Any good orgasm can make you never want to leave that person. This, unfortunately, makes you susceptible to marrying the wrong person. Wedding rings tend to sparkle more when you're horny and sexually connected.

CREATES SOUL TIES

I truly believe that one of the main reasons why God intended for sex to be with your spouse only was because He didn't want you sexually and emotionally tied to someone else other than your spouse. Sex is so powerful, full of passion, fire, love and vulnerability that, when shared with someone not ordained to have it, is extremely dangerous.

I can only imagine how many married men and women are still stuck fantasizing over their past sexual relations. I can only imagine how many still feel emotionally connected because of the sexual vulnerability they once shared with someone else.

DESTROYS WHAT GOD PUT TOGETHER

If you know, without a shadow of a doubt, the person you're dating is your God-ordained spouse, you have even more reason to keep the relationship sexually pure and build it on solid foundation (godliness). Any time that foundation is replaced by sexual impurities, you become like the foolish man in Matthew 7:26-27 (NIV), *"...who built his house on sand,"* and it couldn't withstand the storms of life.

I was that foolish man once. Prior to marrying my wife, our relationship *started* on a solid foundation. When the enemy tried to destroy what God put together, it didn't work. But, when we allowed sexual sin to creep in, our foundation became like sand. When the enemy came striking again, we couldn't stand. We broke up. For that reason, I urge you to build your relationship on a solid foundation of sexual purity so that it can weather any storm.

How to Keep Your Relationship Sexually Pure

For the most part, many Christian couples desire to keep sexual purity in their relationship. However, they fail to do so because they have no protective measures in place. Below, I've created a list of protective measures that will help you be tactical in achieving sexual purity in your relationship.

1. Set boundaries.

A boundary serves as a line or parameter that marks off forbidden areas that could potentially lead to danger. Some of these boundaries may include things you will not do, places you will not go, conversations you will not have, and anything else that could possibly lead you two into sexual sin. If you don't create a list of boundaries, your chances of crossing the forbidden lines of sexual sin will increase tremendously!

In my dating life, I crossed the lines of sexual sin all of the time because I had no boundary letting me know when I was nearing ungodly territory. Had there been a warning point set up to say, "Dane. Stop. You've come too far," I would've at least thought twice before moving forward. Sometimes, all it takes is a second thought to turn you around and lead you back to the safe zone.

2. Be careful when hanging out alone.

If you read *Young and Saved* (my last book), you remember that I recommended that dating couples should never be "home alone" together. My mind still hasn't changed on that. But I believe even now that you must be extra careful in public settings, too. Again, this is coming from someone who broke all the rules and, sadly, I didn't even need to have my girlfriend at my house alone to do so. When you're horny, it's possible for sexual sin to take place anywhere.

Pre-marital sex is selfish.

Nevertheless, I do understand the importance of dating alone and learning about the person you are dating. It's just best to do this in open environments filled with light and people. Try to also stay away from late night hangouts because sexual hormones tend to flare up mostly at night. Finally, instead of hanging out alone all of the time, consider extending an invitation to your accountability partners. If you guys don't have accountability partners, let's look at why your relationship definitely needs them.

3. Have Accountability Partners.

If there's one thing that I wish my wife and I had throughout our dating years, it would've been accountability partners. Yes, my parents called and checked on me often. But they went to bed at 10 p.m., and that's the time I *really* needed accountability. Those were the moments when I needed a friend to call or text me late at night to ensure that I was at home *alone* in my bed. Accountability like that could have helped keep me from sin.

Furthermore, accountability partners also serve as great people to have group dates with. I'd rather end my group date night sin-free instead of alone and repenting with my significant other. This leads me to my next point. You would never have to worry about ending dates sin-free if you two limited your "physical" affection.

NOTE: When the group date ends, your date ends, too. Go home alone.

4. Don't be too physical.

I know it's hard not to be extra touchy. It's hard not to snuggle up, especially when your significant other is looking good. But, touching too much is one of the fastest ways to find yourself in sin. This is why couples must really consider how much physical affection is necessary. More specifically, couples must discuss if whether or not kissing is works for them. Before getting into that though, let's look at what 1300 people voted for on a survey I recently conducted regarding dating and courting, and couples kissing.

Survey questions via Instagram (@ChristianSexEd)

SURVEY QUESTION 1.

"SHOULD DATING/COURTING COUPLES KISS (PECK)?"
Results: 69% (900 people) said that they should kiss.
On the contrary, 31% (400 people) said that they should not kiss.

SURVEY QUESTION 2.

"SHOULD DATING/COURTING COUPLES MAKE OUT?"
Results: 35% (457 people) said couples should make out.
On the contrary, 65% (843 people) said couples should not make out.

The above survey results weren't too shocking to me. It's quite apparent that dating/courting couples shouldn't make out because it's hard to stop when your tongue is in their mouth. Nonetheless, I really want to address the 65% percent of people who said that dating/courting couples should peck. Personally, I understand why so many people approve of this. After all, it's human nature to feel a special connection with someone and to desire to kiss them. However, ask yourself one thing: Do you have enough self-control to stop at a peck? Many have tried, but many have also failed and fell into sin because of a few little pecks.

I'm not saying that a little peck on the lips is wrong at all. But instead, be cautious in all that you do because lust is never satisfied. Therefore, it's essential that you both know your limits and communicate them to each other. If you two can't handle a kiss, come up with other creative ways to display your affection that doesn't involve all of the kissing and touching. The only time that touching is okay is when you're holding hands to pray – just kidding. On a serious note, though, prayer is the driving force that'll help keep your relationship pure.

5. Establish a Prayer Life with the Person You Are Dating

Matthew 18:20 (NIV) says, *For where two or three gather in my name, there am I with them*. If you desire to set the tone of purity in your relationship, invite Jesus to dwell with you two. His presence alone will fight against the urges of sexual sin. It's going to be so much harder to fall into sexual sin when the atmosphere is consumed with God's presence. It's God's presence that gives birth to purity. It's God's presence that *Lead her to prayer,* combats sexual fantasies, temptations *not your bedroom.* and demons of lust! Matter of fact, a couple that doesn't pray together definitely can't slay a demon of sexual impurity together! A common denominator for a relationship's sexual impurity is always a lack of prayer. However, you can beat sexual impurity in your relationship by praying together and following the steps below on how to bring purity back into a relationship!

How to Bring Purity Back Into the Relationship

Purity will never be reestablished back into a relationship until the two of you have *the talk*. This talk might be a little awkward or uncomfortable. It can be hurtful, but this issue of impurity must be verbally addressed. In this talk, the two of you will have to sit down and decide if you guys want to pursue purity together. This can be difficult, especially if he or she isn't on board with the decision.

Moreover, if they aren't on board with pursuing purity together, you will have to end the relationship entirely. If you do decide to stay in this unequally yoked relationship, you will fall into sin again. At some point, they will try to pressure you into doing something you don't want to do, or make you feel bad for rejecting their advances. They may even try to "turn you on" so that you fall right back into sin with them.

On the other hand, if they choose to pursue purity with you, the next step for you two is to repent, turn away from the sin, and ask God to cleanse you two from all sin. Through confession, your sins are forgiven, and you're purified from unrighteousness (1 John 1:9). Purification from the relationship's sexual impurities is needed to move forward.

After receiving purification and forgiveness from God, you two now need to ask each other for forgiveness because you both robbed each other of purity and led a child of God down a path of sin. You'd be surprised at how much power there is in asking the person you led astray to forgive you. Not only will it free you from your sin, but they'll love you even more because they realize that you care about their soul and where they'll spend eternity. That kind of love and forgiveness is a major key to victory.

The next step for you two is to develop a strategy to prevent future falling. Identify the actions that led you two into sexual sin. Once identified, it's simple. Stay far away from the actions that led you two down the path of sin.

For example, if hanging out alone in the car at night led you two into sin, don't do it again. Too often, couples never escape the cycle of sexual sin because they keep doing the same things that got them into sexual sin in the first place. At some point, you have to realize that if it knocked you down before, it can do it again. But, if you two take these precautions, and follow the below eight steps to bring purity back, your chances of falling into sin will lower! Once sexual sin is no longer a problem in your relationship, you two will finally get to enjoy the great gift of purity!

8 Steps to Bringing Purity Back

1. Have the talk. Communicate the issue.
2. Make a mutual decision to stop. If it's not mutual, end the relationship.
3. Repent and ask for forgiveness from God.
4. Offer forgiveness to your significant other and receive it, as well.

5. Acknowledge what led to sin.
6. Set realistic boundaries.
7. Have accountability partners.
8. Grow in God together.

Class Wrap-Up (The Great Gift of Purity)

Other than remaining in good standing with God, the great gift of purity is that you get to know the person God has placed in your life. How beautiful it is to get to know your God-ordained future spouse. The butterflies, shyness and awkward moments of the relationship are truly unforgettable. Then, as time goes on, your relationship begins to deepen, and true love begins to awaken. What a shame it would be to allow sexual sin to mess up that good God-established relationship!

As I mentioned earlier, my wife and I allowed sexual sin to mess our relationship up. To this day, I regret those moments of sin, because I spent time damaging her soul when I could've been listening to her beautiful laugh and tapping into her beautiful mind.

Therefore, instead of longing for sex, long for deep, intimate, godly and intellectual conversations. I'll never forget the days where my girlfriend (who is my wife now) and I remained holy. We didn't have slip-ups. Instead, we conversed for hours about God, our dreams, food, our lives and our future. Those days were beautiful. I would leave with a feeling full of bliss, like I'd just dived into her mind. I got to know her on a deeper level than sex. That was better than any orgasm. It's those beautiful moments that God has planned for you and your future spouse—moments of true love that is sin-free.

10 Commandments of Relationship Purity

1. Judge by the spirit, not your genitals.
2. Lead her to prayer, not your bedroom.
3. Open her veil before you open her legs.
4. Pre-marital sex is selfish.
5. If they love you, they won't fornicate with you.

6. Don't fornicate your way into marriage. You'll start off on a bad foot.
7. Married sex is the only safe sex.
8. There is more to marriage than sex. Do not rush into it because you're horny.
9. A truly godly man won't ask you for naked pictures.
10. No orgasm is worth your soul.

NOTE: A random sexual thought popping in your head isn't sin. It's only sin when you ruminate on it or generate it. In other words, what you do with the random sexual thought determines whether it's going to be a sin or not.

THE SEED

Seed Planted

When a seed is planted into soil, there are two things that can take place. The seed can die, or it can live. If the seed lives, its first goal is to grow stable roots. Roots are what hold everything together and bring life to the seed. Interestingly, this tiny seed that's been planted in the soil has the potential to become the size of a giant tree. In like manner, let me tell you a story of how a tiny seed of lust planted within me blossomed into a giant tree.

My Story

I was ten years old when a seed of lust was planted within me. I remember the day like it was yesterday. I went over to my friend's house after school. As soon as we walked into his room, he said, "Let's watch this video on my computer." I could tell by the tone of his voice that it wasn't going to be a video my parents would approve of. Nonetheless, I didn't know what to expect.

Hesitantly, I said, "Okay."

He then searched through a few computer files. When he finally found the video, he looked back at me with a serious grin and hit play!

To my complete shock, the video was full-blown pornography. It was like nothing I'd ever seen before. I had never watched someone have sex. What I saw that day sexually intrigued me. In a moment, I was sexually awakened. After watching that video, I couldn't help but wonder what sex felt like. I had to know! I couldn't get that video out of my head! All day long, images of that woman's naked body ran through my mind. To be honest, I desperately wanted to have sex with her. But since I couldn't, I found the next best thing. *I masturbated to her.* It was my first time doing this and my first time experiencing sexual pleasure.

Here I was now, a ten-year-old boy who went from knowing nothing to seeing everything. In the matter of a click, I became a porn and masturbation addict. The more I indulged in these behaviors, the more water my seed of lust demanded.

Seed Watered

When a seed touches the soil and makes its way down through itsy bitsy crevices of dirt, it needs one thing in particular to survive. Without it, the seed will die and never sprout. That one thing is water! In order for a seed to grow in the earth, form roots, and create strong roots, water is mandatory.

> *In the matter of a click, I became a porn and masturbation addict.*

Unfortunately, there was never a lack of water on my seed. This led me to experience a little more than a kiss in sixth grade. I was still a virgin, but my hands began to explore. And my conversations got dirtier, as my friends and I stayed up late on AOL Instant Messenger, trying to convince our female classmates to send us naked pictures.

When I finally received my first picture, I was hooked. I can't tell you how many late nights I spent trying to convince her to send me more. It was that picture that summer night that gave my seed enough water to finally sprout.

Seed Sprouts

I can only imagine the excitement a farmer has as he walks outside at the crack of dawn to see his seeds beginning to sprout.

After days of watering, waiting and sunlight, that tiny seed finally developed into something greater.

"Something greater" was the season I began to walk into as I entered high school. No longer was my seed of lust just in the ground. It finally started to break past the soil and sprout as I lost my virginity in my sophomore year. I didn't plan on losing it then. I actually planned on waiting for marriage to have sex. But somewhere over the process of watering my lustful seed, those beliefs got watered down and a tree grew up.

Fully Grown

In order for a tree to become fully grown (reach adulthood), it starts as a seed. It then develops roots, sprouts through the soil and, forms a tree trunk. Finally, it grows a crown. As the crown grows, long and strong branches begin to form and provide shade. The crown developing is the third stage of tree life, which is considered the prime time.

I was at the start of my junior year of high school, which I considered to be my prime time. That year, I hit a new realm in my sexual sin. I became more sexually active. Recklessly and out of control, I'd hook up with multiple women a week. Without any conviction, I ran wild, like a dog without a leash, chasing every cat that "meowed."

You would've thought I'd have some conviction. After all, I sat in the front row of church every Sunday. I even had godly parents giving me counsel regularly. But I chose not to listen because I enjoyed my sin. There was something about getting women that made me feel alive. Like I was the man of the town.

Then, one day during my senior year, something finally hit me. *Conviction!* It came randomly after I finished having sex with a woman. I didn't know what I was feeling at first. I just knew that she had to go. So inwardly, I begged her, *Please put on your clothes because something doesn't feel right.*

When she finally put both legs through her leggings, I blew a sigh of relief. I then walked her downstairs, opened the garage, and said, "I'll text you later." As soon as that garage door shut, I ran upstairs, went into the bathroom and jumped into the shower. The shower was the closest thing to a baptismal pool, and I had to wash the sin off me. I guess I was hoping the water shooting through the showerhead would grant me some spiritual cleansing. That didn't work, though. I was now just a wet sinner.

From that moment on, I was hit with extreme conviction after I had sex. Therefore, I promised God that I wouldn't do it again until I was married. That promise was quickly broken. I did have some slight success, though.

It came two months later when I had the chance to have sex with the same woman mentioned above. Instead of meeting with her at my house for sex, like normal, I took her to a restaurant to eat. We enjoyed ourselves. But once I paid the bill, there was an awkward pause. We didn't know what to do next. I could tell by the look in her eyes that she wanted to come over. I desperately wanted her to, as well. But, I chose the high road and walked her outside. I said, "I'll text you later."

As she walked away, I looked at her butt and instantly regretted not taking her home. Nevertheless, I let her keep walking because the conviction after sex was too much to bear. So, alone I stood there in the parking lot. I was finally considering cutting down the old tree of lust.

I had to wash the sin off me.

Timber

One of the hardest parts about cutting down a tree is getting through the trunk of it. The trunk is composed of these five layers of strength:

1. **OUTER BARK:** Guards the tree from insects and cold weather.
2. **INNER BARK:** Passes food through the tree.
3. **CAMBIUM CELL:** Grows and produces bark.
4. **SAPWOOD:** Funnels water to the tree.
5. **HEARTWOOD:** The most central part of a tree that provides strength, stability and balance.

NOTE: The only way to cut through these layers is with a chainsaw.

Two months into college, and a few more hookups later, I realized that I needed that chainsaw. Enough was enough. It was time to remove this tree of lust. So, I allowed God to cut through these five layers.

1. **MY GUARD:** Kept me from letting God in.
2. **FEMALE CONNECTIONS:** Allowed my tree of lust to keep growing.
3. **PRIDE:** Funneled lust water to my sexual sin.
4. **ALBUMS OF NAKED PICTURES:** This was the hardest layer to cut through. Though I loved those photos, I couldn't have peace with them on my phone. So, one night, I mustered up enough courage and deleted all naked pictures from my phone. Subsequently, I took it a step further. I went and grabbed a memory card full of more photos and broke it in half as a declaration that I wouldn't go back to that sin. It hurt so bad deleting those photos. The peace I felt afterward eventually made up for it, though.
5. **MY HEART:** The last layer God cut through was my *heart,* which had been set on pleasing my flesh sexually and getting the most women. As God cut through this layer, my heart started to desire Jesus more and women less. This led me to make the greatest decision of my life on September 25, 2011.

During that Sunday morning service altar call, I heard God's audible voice for the first time in my life. Loudly, He said, "Dane." Nervous, and with my heart pounding, I responded, and I made my way down to the altar room. I prayed to receive the baptism of the Holy Spirit, which is the infilling of God's spirit that comes with speaking in tongues. I didn't get it that day. With a heart made up for God, though, I came back to church three days later and received the Holy Spirit. I spoke in tongues as the first apostles did in Acts 2:4, over 2000 years ago. This infilling of God's spirit was the final saw through my tree of lust. And, for the first time in my life, I felt *somewhat* free from the grips of lust. It was now my responsibility to *keep* myself free. I had to make a choice. I had to water the new spirit within me, or I could water what should have been dead.

Watering What Should Be Dead

When a tree is cut down, all food production is taken away. In saving efforts, the tree will send out water sprouts. If you don't want this tree to grow again, you will need to cut the water sprouts weekly.

With the Holy Spirit, I now had the power to cut away the sprouts of lust. However, I couldn't get over this awkward feeling. At times, I was full of excitement for the things of God. Then other times, I would randomly feel like something was missing.

It was the little lust devils that I spent the majority of my life entertaining. They were gone, and I had to deal with a new emptiness. Although I should've been rejoicing that they were gone, I found myself reminiscing over the memories we had.

The more I reminisced, the more lust grew back. This led me back to a life of sexual sin. To be specific, I wasn't having sex all the time, or wilding out, because I couldn't allow anyone to know that this new "holy roller" was sinning. Instead, I went to my secret place of sin: *masturbation and pornography*. My late nights consisted of either reading the Word of God or masturbating to live sex cams. These inconsistencies hindered my walk with God, putting me in a cycle of sexual sin for almost four years. I would move forward with God five steps, then fall back three steps to lust.

No matter how much I prayed, fasted and read the Word, I couldn't break the cycle. This frustration of being saved, and wanting to grow in God, yet feeling incapable to do so, killed me. I felt hopeless. That was, until God spoke something to my spirit that opened doors of deliverance.

He said, "You are in complete control of your deliverance from lust. It won't start though until you say, 'No,' to every temptation."

So, that's exactly what I did. On Facebook and Instagram, I unfollowed, unfriended and blocked all the women, and their pages, that would tempt me. Then, in grocery stores or at the gym, if I saw a woman with a nice body, I'd go the opposite way so I could avoid lusting after her. As extreme as this was, it kept my eyes on Jesus, not women. These behavior changes—coupled with a few steps from *110: Prison Break*—freed me from the spirit of lust.

Class Wrap-Up

Being freed from lust is amazing. Let's not get it twisted, though. Maintaining freedom from lust isn't easy. Nonetheless, this battle with our eyes can be won with wisdom.

That wisdom is to protect your deliverance from lust at all costs. If the computer causes you to sin, throw it out. If your phone tempts you every night, turn it off. If Snapchat is your demise, delete it. If certain pages on Instagram tempt you, block them. Basically, run from anything that can bring you into the bondage of lust.

I've managed to hold onto my deliverance by using this wisdom and allowing God to pour out more of His spirit within me. The more God's spirit pours into me, the more lustful mess clears out of me.

It's God's spirit that can cleanse us from any and all lust. If we get our daily dose of it, we can stay free. I want to stay free from lust, and I don't want my deliverance to be in vain. If you feel the same way, fight with everything in you to stay free from lust so you can enjoy this walk with Jesus.

THE LUST CHECK

To observe the amount of sinful lust we intake, I created a lust checklist. I did so because, unknowingly, seeds of lust are being planted within us. It's these seeds that later blossom into a tree and, eventually, overtake us.

If you answer, **"YES"** to any of the following questions, keep a tally of your points.

1. Do you have sex dreams more than once a week? *(10 points)*
2. Do you listen to music with sexual lyrics? *(10 points)*
3. If single, is sex your sole purpose for desiring marriage? *(20 points)*
4. If married, is sex the best thing about marriage? *(20 points)*
5. When someone with a nice body walks by, do you look? *(25 points)*
6. When you scroll past something sexual on social media, do you pause and look at it? *(25 points)*
7. Do you watch television shows with nudity? *(40 points)*
8. Do you keep your eyes open when nudity comes on TV? *(50 points)*
9. Do you daydream about sex? *(60 points)*
10. Do you ponder on your previous sexual experiences? *(70 points)*
11. Do you watch pornography? *(100 points)*
12. Do you masturbate? *(120 points)*
13. Do you engage in sexting? *(125 points)*
14. Are you participating in any pre-marital sexual activity? *(150 points)*
15. If married, are you having a physical affair? *(175 points)*

TALLY SHEET TOTAL	1000 POINTS
No Lust Problem	0
Slight Problem	1-100
Moderate Problem	101-200
High Problem	201-300
Severe Problem	301-450
Serious Deliverance Needed	451-700
Danger Zone	701-1000

This test wasn't to condemn you, but to show you how much lust we have in our lives at times. Whether you scored "Moderate Problem" or "Danger Zone," all sinful lust is dangerous. Never become cozy in any amount of sinful lust, because it has the power to grow exceedingly fast and take you out.

108
SEXUAL DREAMS

A hh, it wasn't real!

Disappointed, I woke up, realizing that it was only a sex dream, not a real-life experience. Left turned on from the dream, I needed to find a way to release this sexual pressure. *Guess I'll take matters into my own hands*, I thought. Literally.

This has been the outcome of sexual dreams for many others, too. Approximately 76% of the 1,000 people I surveyed via @ChristianSexEd reported that sexual dreams have led them into sexual sin (masturbation, pornography, foreplay, fornication, adultery, sexual lust, etc.) Those results were staggering, proving to us that sexual dreams have the power to influence individuals into making sinful sexual decisions.

SEXUAL DREAMS
Dreams of a sexual nature that can include having sex, watching sex, pursuing sex, and/or reliving past sexual experiences.

Sexual dreams do this by giving you a taste of your wildest fantasies in an altered state of consciousness, so much so that the experience feels real. Dreams are the closest feelings to reality. It's hard to experience the orgasmic high of a wet dream and not be affected by it when you wake up. These dreams can then dictate your conscious actions and give birth to ungodly sexual behaviors, curiosities, fantasies and explorations.

But, what is the reason behind these dirty dreams?

Are we the sole culprit?

Could there be something bigger working against us?

Today, I want to answer those questions and give you two reasons why we have these dreams. The first reason we have these types of dreams is because of *ourselves*. In the latter portion of this chapter, we'll discuss how to be free from ourselves. Secondly, one of the most overlooked reasons behind sexual dreams is demons. We must address the possibility of some sexual dreams being sourced from the enemy as a sexual assault.

Demons & Sex Dreams

I don't know about you, but I've had some intense sex dreams, which left me feeling violated. It was as if I was being seduced in my sleep. The best way to describe it is that it felt like an attack from hell. The only problem in past times was that I didn't know where these dreams came from. I did lust a lot, but there was no way they all could've stemmed from that. Something was still off.

Therefore, one day, I asked myself, *Could these dreams possibly be a spiritual attack from Satan?* I knew that Satan

> **WET DREAMS**
> When an individual dreams about something sexual while involuntarily ejaculating fluid from their genitals, without any masturbation occurring.

had a measure of power. I just didn't know if he had enough to get into my dreams. What made this thought of demons possibly infiltrating my dreams even more challenging was that I couldn't find any scriptural evidence of it. If I could find evidence, then I'd know they were, at times, responsible for our sexual dreams. Eager to find out, I studied this matter. Eventually, I was pointed to a few verses in the book of Job, which gave me the scriptural proof that demons can, in fact, infiltrate your dreams. In order to prove this though, we must look at the context of Job's story first.

The Bible tells us that Job was a righteous man and that, there was no one on earth like him (Job 1:8). God then finds Job fit enough to go through a few tragic things. For the betterment of Job, God allows Satan to attack Job's life. Subsequently, Satan's goal was to get Job to curse God. He tried to accomplish this by killing

Job's servants, children and his livestock. He also struck him with painful boils, leaving Job in a state of tragedy. This led three of Job's friends to come down and mourn with him for seven days.

When those days were up, Job cried out because of his anguish and sorrow. And imminently, Job's friend—Eliphaz—responded with something that led me to believe that demons can give you dreams.

Eliphaz and Part of His Dream

Job 4:12-18 (MSG)
A word came to me in secret—
a mere whisper of a word, but I heard it clearly.
It came in a scary dream one night,
after I had fallen into a deep, deep sleep.
Dread stared me in the face, and Terror.
I was scared to death—I shook from head to foot.
A spirit glided right in front of me—
the hair on my head stood on end.
I couldn't tell what it was that appeared there—
a blur . . . and then I heard a muffled voice:
"How can mere mortals be more righteous than God?
How can humans be purer than their Creator?
Why, God doesn't even trust his own servants,
doesn't even cheer his angels."

As we break down Eliphaz's response, we see that a word was given to him in a "scary dream" during a "deep sleep" by a "spirit" that glided in front of him. This text lets us know that a spirit hijacked Eliphaz's dream and whispered this word to him. However, was that spirit from God or a demon?

Here are a few reasons why I believe it was a demon:

1. There was nothing about the spirit that indicated it was from God. Whenever the Bible talks about a spirit being from God, it's clearly indicated. (e.g., Spirit of God, Holy Spirit, God's spirit, etc.)

2. The spirit utters words that indicate this message wasn't from God, but a bitter demon.

God does not trust his own angels and has charged his messengers with foolishness (Job 4:18, NLT).

We know the spirit in the dream spoke falsely because, throughout the Bible, God does indeed trust His messengers (angels), and has given them serious tasks, as well. Angels were used to lead Lot and his family out of Sodom. Then, an angel (Gabriel) was used to tell Mary about Jesus being born. Lastly, an angel will be used to seize the devil in the Book of Revelation, proving that God does trust His angels.

3. In the latter part of Job 4:18 NLT, the spirit says that God, "charged his messengers with foolishness." Only a demon would say something like that. Moreover, this passage is likely referring to God kicking Satan and one-third of the angels out of heaven. God didn't charge them with foolishness; instead, He charged them with sin because they were wicked.

4. One of the main reasons I know that the spirit that was speaking wasn't from God is because of God's rebuke against Eliphaz in Job 42:7 ESV, which says,

The Lord said to Eliphaz the Temanite: "My anger burns against you and against your two friends, for you have not spoken of me what is right, as my servant Job has." God would have never rebuked Eliphaz's words had he been speaking on behalf of Him.

With this overwhelming evidence, we can see that Eliphaz's dream and interpretation of it in Job 4:1 — Job 5:27 was received from a spirit that was not of God (demon), with a goal to deceive Job. How did the demon hope to deceive Job? Simply by having Eliphaz believe that the dream was from God, revealing that Job was being punished because of his unrighteousness. But, we know that Eliphaz's dream was contrary to what God was saying because Job wasn't in sin.

God said this about Job: *"There is no one on earth like him;*

he is blameless and upright, a man who fears God and shuns evil" (Job 2:3, NIV). Therefore, since Eliphaz's dream was contrary to what God was saying, the dream couldn't have been from God. Instead, it had to be from a spirit (demon) of Satan, hoping to get Job to curse God. This proves to us that demons can:

A. Give us dreams
B. Speak to us in dreams
C. Influence us through dreams

These things being considered, I believe demons have been going under the radar and attacking us sexually at our most vulnerable state: when we sleep. Since they have remained under radar, many have stayed under bondage because they don't know where these dreams are coming from. After all, how can you fight a war without knowing who your enemy is?

But now, since we've exposed who our enemy is, let's find out how to overcome the attacks.

Fighting Sexual Dreams from Demons

Before attempting to fight, we must first know that this battle is spiritual. Ephesians 6:12 (NKJV says, *For we do not wrestle against flesh and blood, but against principalities, against powers, against the rulers of the darkness of this age, against spiritual hosts of wickedness in the heavenly places.*

Further reading of Ephesians 6 reveals that there is a spiritual realm, where demons dwell. It's the place where they launch fiery attacks. These attacks can be dreams. In order for us to combat them, we must apply the full armor of God mentioned in Ephesians 6:11-18.

This armor is broken up into six pieces. However, there are three pieces I would like to highlight: the shield of faith, the sword of the spirit, and the breastplate of righteousness (Ephesians 6:14-17, NLT). These three (as well as the three not listed) will help you overcome the enemy's attacks and, in this case, overcome sexual dreams from demons.

The first piece of armor is the shield of faith, which will *quench all of the fiery darts of the wicked one* (Ephesians 6:16, NKJV). It's through our faith that God protects us with His power (1 Peter 1:5, NLT). In other words, our faith couples with God's power, which activates a shield in the spirit against the fiery darts (sexual dreams) of the enemy. The more we increase in faith, the stronger this shield becomes and the less affected we are by Satan's darts. We can grow in faith by putting our full trust in God and using the authority He has given over demons (Luke 10:19).

Coupled with faith, the next piece of armor is the sword of the Spirit. According to Ephesians 6:17, this is the Word of God. Moreover, the Word of God *is alive and active, sharper than any double-edged sword*, with the power to demolish the works of hell (Hebrews 4:12, NIV). We know this because, every time Satan tempted Jesus in the wilderness, Jesus used the Word of God to overcome the attack! If you want to dismantle Satan's attacks of sexual dreams, you must declare the Word of God over your sleep, dreams and life. For example, you could say, "The Lord rebukes you, Satan!" I declare lust-free dreams, in Jesus' name (Zechariah 3:2, NIV)!

You must declare the Word of God over your sleep.

The third piece of armor is the breastplate of righteousness (Ephesians 6:14).

In a matter of war, a soldier would be foolish to not wear a breastplate, as it is used to protect vital organs. One arrow to your torso without the breastplate and you're dead. The same logic applies to Christians in spiritual warfare. Without the breastplate of righteousness, you leave yourself vulnerable to the enemy's attacks. If, and when a fiery dart (sexual dream) from the enemy lands, you can easily spiritually succumb to the injuries. But, if you wear this righteousness that is first received by faith in Christ (Romans 3:22), the darts (dreams) can't get through this breastplate, which is made of spiritual steel. Moreover, we put this righteousness on by walking in the ways of Jesus Christ. Our righteousness through living holy becomes a weapon against the enemy.

It's Not All Demons: Check Yourself

Though we have armor that gives us strength to fight against Satan's attacks, we must realize that we, at times, are the sole culprit for our sexual dreams. Don't get me wrong. You can blame demons for a great deal of mess because they're often responsible. However, before blaming demons, examine yourself and what you're taking in. Your dreams just may be a result of your daily actions. I'll use myself as an example. In past times, I would drool in lust over women all day. Then, at night, I would dream of them sexually. My sexual dreams were the output of my lustful input. In other words, if you keep taking in lustful things, you'll keep on having lustful dreams.

However, if you desire to have pure dreams, then you must in take pure things. This includes pure music, movies, television shows and conversations. The purest of all is the Word of God. Read the Word of God throughout the day, but even more so at night before going to bed. The Word will renew, sanctify and purify your mind—setting you up for a pure dream.

Class Wrap-Up

As we saw throughout today's lesson, having pure dreams isn't entirely easy because you're fighting against demons and your sinful nature. However, though it may not be easy, it's not impossible, if you use the weapons God has given you and take in things of a pure nature. Doing this will help set you free and keep your free from sexual dreams! Amen!

POP QUIZ

CHAPTER 108 QUIZ

1. Who received a dream from a demon?

2. The whole armor of God, which can be used to fight against sexual dreams, is found in what chapter of Ephesians?

A. Chapter 4
B. Chapter 5
C. Chapter 1
D. Chapter 6

3. In what chapter of Job does Eliphaz receive a dream from a demon?

A. Chapter 1
B. Chapter 3
C. Chapter 4
D. Chapter 5

4. What percentage of the 1,000 people surveyed said that, "Sexual dreams led them into sexual sin"?

A. 49%
B. 87%
C. 76%
D. 69%

5. Why did Satan give Eliphaz a dream?

A. To deceive Job
B. To get Job to curse God
C. To have Eliphaz thinking that Job was unrighteous
D. All of the above

CHAPTER 108 QUIZ ANSWERS

1. Who received a dream from a demon?

Answer: Eliphaz

2. The whole armor of God, which can be used to fight against sexual dreams is found in what chapter of Ephesians?

A. Chapter 4
B. Chapter 5
C. Chapter 1
D. Chapter 6

Answer: D – Chapter 6 (Ephesians 6:11)

3. In what chapter of Job does Eliphaz receive a dream from a demon?

A. Chapter 1
B. Chapter 3
C. Chapter 4
D. Chapter 5

Answer: C – Chapter 4

4. What percentage of the 1,000 people surveyed said that, "Sexual dreams led them into sexual sin"?

A. 49%
B. 87%
C. 76%
D. 69%

Answer: C – 76%

5. Why did Satan give Eliphaz a dream?

A. To deceive Job
B. To get Job to curse God
C. To have Eliphaz thinking that Job was unrighteous
D. All of the above

Answer: D – All of the above

109

DIRTY HANDS

OVERCOMING MASTURBATION

It was 9 a.m. I hopped on my computer upstairs and started watching porn, while I masturbated. Then, all of a sudden, I heard the front door unlock. Immediately, my heart dropped because I was home alone. I pulled up my pants quickly, exited out of the computer screen, and rushed to my room. Turns out, a relative, who had been staying with us at the time, forgot something at home and came back to get it. It was one of the scariest moments of my life because I thought my deep, dark secret was going to come to the light.

If we're honest with ourselves, many people reading this have had similar stories with masturbation. And although many people (especially Christians) are struggling with masturbation, it's still a topic that everyone is afraid to talk about. It's as if the word *masturbation* has become taboo in the church. Take a minute and think about the last time you heard the word *masturbation* mentioned in church. I would be willing to bet that it's been quite a while for most of you! Personally, I've only heard masturbation addressed two times at church in my life, which is sad. For that reason, in today's lesson, we're going to talk about everything you need to know about masturbation— first starting with the statistics.

Statistics on Masturbation

To find out how many people have struggled with masturbation at some point in their life, I recently ran a survey on my Instagram page (@ChristianSexEd).

85% of Christians have struggled with masturbation.

[500 respondents]
(Survey via @ChristianSexEd Instagram)

SURVEY QUESTION 1

The first survey question asked to Christians and non-Christians was, **"HAVE YOU EVER STRUGGLED WITH MASTURBATION?"**

Out of the 500 people who responded, 425 (85%) said, "Yes," they have struggled with masturbation before. Approximately 75 people (15%) said, "No," they have never struggled with masturbation.

To put those numbers in perspective, if you went to a mall and shook hands with ten people, you can guarantee that more than eight of them have struggled with masturbation at some point in their life.

SURVEY QUESTION 2

For our next survey question, we surveyed 500 Christians. The point was to see if masturbation is something that currently affects believers, as well. Therefore, we asked them, **"HAVE YOU MASTURBATED IN THE LAST THREE MONTHS?"**

Of those surveyed, 68% (341 people) of Christians that responded to the survey said, "Yes" and 32% (159 people) said, "No."

The above survey results reveal to us that more than 68% of Christians are currently still struggling with masturbation. So, the next time you go to church, look at just under three quarters of the members sitting in the sanctuary. You can bet that they are struggling or have recently struggled with masturbation.

SURVEY QUESTION 3

For our last survey question, we reached out to the married community. We did this because many people tend to think that once you get married, your struggle with masturbation will cease. To see if that's true, we asked 100 married men and women this question: **"IN THE LAST FOUR MONTHS, HAVE YOU MASTURBATED?"** Of those surveyed, 46% said, "Yes," and 54% said, "No."

These statistics show us that marriage will not cure your desire to masturbate. If it did, almost half of married individuals wouldn't be masturbating behind their spouse's back. Nevertheless, here's a thought as to why marriage doesn't cure masturbation problems.

As an unmarried person, you may have masturbated twice a day, every day to feed your sexual appetite. By doing that, you set a bar of how much sexual gratification you need. Now, let me break down some honest truth for you. Once you get married, it's likely that you will *not* have sex twice a day. In a lot of cases, married couples hope to have sex twice *a week*! Twice a week is actually considered really good, and most married couples don't even hit that mark. Life happens, kids happen, and work happens, which then means you won't have sex as often as you masturbated before marriage.

So, guess what happens to that bar of sexual gratification that you set with frequent masturbating prior to marriage? It's not met, which leaves you sexually off balance because your body is expecting the same amount of sexual gratification it received in your singleness from masturbation. And since that bar isn't being met, many married individuals will go to their secret room while their spouse is asleep, flip on the porn, and masturbate. Having said that, if you're single and struggling with masturbation, get delivered so you don't take it into your marriage.

Moreover, masturbation has no preference of who it affects. It affects the married, the dating, the single, the Christian and the non-Christian. To add to that list, it affects women, too. Yes, women masturbate, too! I know a lot of people believe that men are horn-dogs and that they are the only ones who masturbate. But, many (if not most) of our masturbation survey respondents were women!

Now that we know that masturbation affects everybody of all genders, and all relationships, let's explore a few reasons why people masturbate.

Why Do People Masturbate?

For starters, we know that people obviously masturbate because they're horny. However, there are several other underlying reasons that play a role in one's masturbation. One of those reasons is stress.

Stress

As a result of being stressed out, masturbation is often a go-to because an orgasm relieves the pressures of life. This is why you'll notice that people tend to masturbate more after long, hard days. Hence, masturbation is the cap of their night, meaning that it helps them seal their day with pleasure and peace. It's the pleasure through masturbation that temporarily detaches them from their problem by allowing them to focus on pleasure.

Sexual Deprivation

One main contributor to masturbation is sexual deprivation, which is simply being or feeling sexually starved. Sexual deprivation takes place in many marriages and relationships. When an individual is sexually deprived, masturbation becomes the outlet to get their sexual fix. Also, when a man or woman feels that their spouse isn't satisfying them sexually, whether it's not *often* enough or *good* enough, he or she may result to taking it into his or her own hands (no pun intended).

Idle Time

Too much time on your hands can lead to you using your hands — literally! When you think about it, a lot of bad decisions are made when a person has nothing to do. This is why parents often encourage their teenage children to stay busy. They know the dangers that they can run into when they have too much idle time. When it comes

> *Too much time on your hands can lead to you using your hands.*

to masturbation, idle time is dangerous because you have time to wander and browse. If you're struggling with lust, this idle time opens the door to pornography, which then leads to masturbation.

Growing up, my idle time was extremely high, especially during summer break. I had the entire house to myself from 8 a.m. to 5:30 p.m. It was hard to stay busy for those nine and a half hours. So much of my idle time turned into watching pornography and masturbating. But on the days that I stayed occupied and had plans in place, I masturbated less. If you want to masturbate less, stay busy and eliminate idle time.

No One Has To Know

People tend to love masturbation because it's their little sexual secret. Since masturbation only involves you and demons, it's often viewed as a safer way to sin. Yes, that's an oxymoron because there is no safe way to sin. All sin leads to death. However, many people will choose masturbation over sexual intercourse because they can get sexual satisfaction without getting pregnant, getting someone else pregnant or catching an STD. Lastly, no one will find out. When you have sex with someone, there's a chance your Christian reputation can be tarnished because someone can find out. But when you have sex with yourself, nobody will know. This is one of the main reasons why people masturbate. They can fulfill their sexual needs without any physical consequences.

From a natural mind, that doesn't seem like a bad reason for masturbating. After all, wouldn't it be nice to please yourself sexually, without consequences? Though that may sound nice, there's one thing that you must ask yourself first: *Is masturbation a sin?*

Is Masturbation a Sin?

When you look throughout all 66 books in the Bible, one word you will not find is masturbation. Since not specifically mentioned, many think that it's not a sin. For those who may believe this, or are unsure if it's a sin or not, I want to offer you two words that I believe often make masturbation a sin: *sinful lust*. As mentioned in *106: Forbidden Lines*, sinful lust is defined as:

> *"The sexual coveting or objectification of someone that you're not married to. Additionally, sexual desires become sinful lust when they willfully manifest through the eyes, imaginations, thoughts, actions and the heart with the intent to gain sexual gratification. In other words, the only person that you can willfully think about or look at in a way that brings you sexual gratification is your spouse of the opposite sex."*

This is lust that's condemned in Job 31:1, and by Jesus in Matthew 5:28. This lust is also typically active during masturbation because one of the following is usually being done simultaneously:

A. Watching pornography
B. Looking at someone with sinful lust
C. Pondering on previous sexual encounters
D. Giving thought to sexual fantasies

All of the above acts are forms of sinful lust. If you do either while masturbating, you are in sin. Nevertheless, many will try to escape that lust so they can continue masturbating. They'll do so by avoiding pornographic material, in hopes that they can masturbate with a lust-free mind. Achieving that is highly doubtful, especially since there's always something in the mind of the person who is masturbating that initially turned them on to masturbate.

Think about it. Masturbation is done for sexual gratification. What usually makes you want sexual gratification? Typically, something sexual. Quite often, it's one's sinful desires.

Furthermore, since the goal of masturbation is to achieve an orgasm, we must ask the question: Will a lust-free mind help accomplish that goal? I don't think so. But, a lust-filled mind, fixated on sexual fantasies, will. This is because masturbation is a sexual act that's done when someone is sexually aroused, typically through sinful lust.

Lastly, there is one Scripture regarding sinful lust that may be "somewhat" condemning the act of masturbation. It's found in Matthew 5:30 (NKJV), which says, *And if your right hand causes you to sin, cut it off and cast it from you; for it is more profitable for you that one of your members perish, than for your whole body to be cast in hell.*

I've read that Scripture several times in my life. But, recently, the thought hit me: *Could Jesus be condemning the act of masturbation here?*

After all, the whole basis of Matthew 5:27-32 is lust and adultery. Jesus first condemns sinfully lusting after a woman in Matthew 5:28-29. In the next sentence, with a premise of lust, He condemns using the hand for sin. I beg to ask the question, "What's one of the primary things that the hand couples with lust to sin?" Masturbation. People masturbate with their hand far more often than they use their hand to commit any other sexual sin. Nevertheless, we don't know for sure if masturbation is being condemned here, but it's a possibility. But, even if Matthew 5:30 isn't specifically about masturbation, the sinful lust depicted in Matthew 5:28 will almost always make masturbation a sin.

If only I'd heard about the lust of Matthew 5:28 growing up, just maybe, I wouldn't have masturbated so much. Anyhow, since I did masturbate so much, and I struggled with it for so many years, it's only right that I share my short story with you!

A Slave to Masturbation

As mentioned in *Chapter 106: Where It All Started*, the first time I ever masturbated, I was ten years old. I didn't stop masturbating until I was twenty-two years old. Yes, I spent twelve years as a slave to masturbation. During those years I masturbated almost every day for hours on end. There was even a time, when I was twelve, that I slightly masturbated during class under my desk after being turned on from a girl's underwear.

It's safe to say that I was addicted. Masturbation was my deadly drug of choice. Just like the drug addict knows the consequences, yet still goes for the needle, I still chose masturbation.

Every night when that clock hit 10 p.m., I thought about whether

I would masturbate that night or not. While that question kept me momentarily paralyzed, a million thoughts ran through my head.

If I masturbate, I'm going to hate myself tomorrow.
I preach next Wednesday night, and this is going to taint my anointing.
I have church tomorrow morning. What if I can't feel God's presence?
I don't want to disappoint God.

Then, the last thought before I caved into masturbation was, *This is the last time.*

Then, boom.
I grabbed the lotion.
I turned the lights off.
I pulled my pants down.
I turned on some porn.
And I masturbated.

My body knew these five steps far too well…until June 2, 2016. That was the last day I would ever follow those steps. It was two days before I got married. After that night of masturbation, I told myself, *I can't take this demon into my marriage.* The last thing I would ever want to do is confess to my wife that I was watching porn and masturbating. I had already broken her heart in the past with lies, so I knew that would, too. That day had to be my *last day.*

However, like I mentioned earlier, marriage doesn't cure your desire to masturbate. You don't just pop on a ring and poof! Masturbation desires are gone! That would've been nice. I actually hoped for that, but my desire to masturbate was still there. Nevertheless, I didn't give in because I wanted to be faithful to God and my wife. It was probably the hardest thing in my life to do. Below are some steps that I took that helped me overcome masturbation. They are what helped me stay free for, presently, three years and eleven months.

How to Overcome Masturbation

1. Break the Habit.

Freedom from masturbation will only take place when you make up your mind to break the habit completely. In order for this to happen, you will have to go cold turkey from masturbation. You can't try to wean yourself off of masturbation. You must break the dependency that your body has on masturbation by rejecting it daily. This daily rejection will help you gain power over masturbation. With each day that goes by, you'll get stronger, and eventually, your desire to masturbate will lessen.

2. Pray.

Prayer is single-handedly the most effective weapon in overcoming masturbation. It's through prayer that you can ask God to help you when you're horny. John 15:7 (NIV) says, "*If you remain in me and my words remain in you, ask whatever you wish, and it will be done for you.*"

I'm a living witness that the above Scripture works. Weeks ago, this extreme horniness randomly came over me. This type of horniness that I felt was unusual. What made matters worse was that my wife wasn't near me. This meant I had two options: pray it away or masturbate it away. I chose the first. I asked God to remove the horniness and, almost instantly, it went away. I knew it was God, too, because I felt His presence hover over me and remove the horniness. So, the next time you're tempted to masturbate, pray it away!

3. Have a "trusted" individual pray for you and keep you accountable.

You have to have a *trusted* individual because you don't want your business in the "church streets." If you confide in the wrong individual, or tell too many people, the whole church is going to know that you're struggling with masturbation. Therefore, ask God to link you up with a trusted individual. More specifically, ask for someone who can stand in agreement with you through prayer for your deliverance from masturbation, as well as hold you accountable when you feel weak.

Unfortunately, when I struggled with masturbation, I didn't reach out to anyone at all. To this day, no one (other than my wife) actually knows that, at a point in my life, I struggled with masturbation. After the world reads this, they will know. Nevertheless, I was always too embarrassed to share this issue with anyone. Although I desperately needed prayer and deliverance, I kept it inside, which I don't recommend. Masturbation is something that you don't have to struggle with alone. Reach out to someone. It may be what saves your soul.

4. Set boundaries for yourself.

You know yourself, and you know what your masturbation triggers are! Whatever triggers you, stay away from it. It's simple. If Instagram, Snapchat or certain television shows have been your nightly kryptonite, cut it off early before all seductive things start coming on. If texting certain people after certain hours get your hormones turning, turn your phone off early. Whatever draws you into masturbation, put it on the list and separate yourself from it starting today!

After you make your list, find something to fill in the time that's normally allotted for masturbation. This could be a project you're working on or a hobby. Personally, I liked going to the gym at nighttime to replace the time I would masturbate. The gym worked well for me because I was getting into better shape, filling in my normal masturbation time, and getting myself exhausted before bed, which helped me fall asleep faster and further avoid masturbation. It's these types of boundaries that will give you victory. This big victory today will motivate you for tomorrow's war.

5. Understand that you will burn (be very horny) some nights.

After you've tried to break the habit of masturbation by praying, talking to your accountability partner, and following your boundaries, there will still be some nights that you burn like crazy, and are hornier than ever before! However, you will just have to close your eyes and go to sleep, horny. I know that's going to feel like an impossible task. But once you complete it, there's no better feeling than waking up the next morning to realize that you overcame masturbation the night before.

It's those big victories that change your burn from being sexual to spiritual, which increases your desire for God even more. If that's still not enough to convince you, think about the great peace that you have going to bed, knowing that you're right with God. On the contrast, every time I allowed the burn to lure me into masturbation, I went to bed fearful of the burning hell I could wake up to. But, when I went to sleep without masturbating, I slept in great peace, which was better than any orgasm. Therefore, choose peace over pleasure, and don't masturbate your way to hell, no matter how horny you are.

Class Wrap-Up

As we saw above, there are techniques that can help you overcome masturbation. But, ultimately, the ball is in your court. If you want to break free from masturbation, you can break free. The best part about attempting to break free from masturbation is that you have God helping you. However, God will not break you from this habit alone. You also have to be a willing vessel to fight for your freedom. As you fight and deny your flesh, God will back you up and give you the doses of strength needed to overcome masturbation. Finally, as we end today's lesson, I want to leave you with this story.

After I was done with masturbation, and my mind was made up not to do it, there came a night when I almost fell back into it. I was extremely turned on and I wanted to masturbate so badly. So, I proceeded to get some lotion and go into the shower to masturbate. As I stepped into the shower, I could feel my heart pounding and an aching in my stomach. I was literally fighting the grips of hell. Deep within, I knew the devil was watching me, and that he would be rejoicing at my downfall. I even knew that, if I went back to masturbating, I would stay there. I wouldn't stop. So, I sat there for two minutes, which felt like an eternity, going back and forth in my mind. I kept asking myself, *Is it worth it to masturbate?* Finally, I told myself, "I want God more than I do this pleasure!" I then washed the lotion off my hands and didn't masturbate. Today, someone reading this needs to wash the lotion off of their hands and be completely free from masturbation.

30 Quick Tips to Help You Overcome Masturbation

1. Move your lotion and tissue box to the bathroom.
2. Throw your vibrators and dildos away.
3. Delete the naked pictures from your phone.
4. Put your phone far away from you at night.
5. Download porn-blocking software on your phone and computer.
6. Delete your Snapchat app.
7. Unfollow pages that tempt you.
8. Block people that tempt you on social media.
9. Stop watching shows on TV that tempt you.
10. Install a camera in your room.
11. Sleep with the door open.
12. Set boundaries for yourself.
13. Have someone pray for you.
14. Talk to your accountability partner.
15. Talk to your pastor about your struggle.
16. Spend time with God before going to bed.
17. Read or listen to the Bible before falling asleep.
18. Pray yourself to sleep.
19. Pray in tongues.
20. Listen to Christian music before bed.
21. Eliminate idle time.
22. Work out late at night.
23. Exhaust yourself before you get in bed.
24. Go cold turkey.
25. Walk in the self-control that God gave you.
26. Put your laptop in the living room at night.
27. Sleep with underwear and pants on.
28. Tell your spouse that you're struggling with masturbation.
29. Tell your parents that you're struggling with masturbation.
30. Put on a good "pure" movie before bed.

110
PRISON BREAK

For too long, millions of people have been walking around with shackles on their hands and feet. I can picture a bus picking them up in their orange jumpsuits as they're being hauled away to a facility called *Satan's Prison of Sexual Sin*. Unfortunately, the number of people sentenced to this facility has been growing exceedingly. More people are being sexually imprisoned every day. On the inmates' record sheets, you find charges for sexual sin, such as lust, fornication, adultery, masturbation, incest, homosexuality and bestiality. With a rap sheet of charges so long, it seems as if they'll never be free. It seems as if they will spend the rest of their lives locked up and in sin. If nothing is done, they'll spend their next life locked up, too, for an eternity in hell with flames of fire and torment.

Though this appears to be the fate for many, and a chance at freedom seems farfetched, I still believe this generation of prisoners will experience a mass prison break from these cells of sexual sin!

As exciting as this prison break may sound, I have to break some news to you first. There is a tough warden of this facility named Satan. He will not let this escape be easy. Throughout his facility, guards (demons of lust) stand tasked with one job: Prevent anyone who dares to try to escape.

Having said that, this prison break will be one of the hardest things you ever have to do. There will be times you want to throw in the towel and say, "Forget it!" But don't stop because this fight isn't done alone. You'll have God on your side, and He will equip you with the proper necessary weapons for a successful prison break. Before going over those weapons, let's look at how these prisoners got locked up in the first place.

How One Becomes Imprisoned by Sexual Sin

Many of these prisoners have unique stories of how they got arrested by sexual sin. There's one thing almost all of them have in common: They walked through an open door of temptation. This wasn't by coincidence. It was by the luring of Satan. He has mastered the art of luring people into his cell of sexual sin.

He is successful at luring people in because he uses good bait. Whether it's a sexy person who's interested in you, or a porn video, he'll use something to attract you, hook you, and reel you into his open cell doors. It doesn't stop there, though. That's only half of it. The enemy doesn't only desire to get you into his cell, but his ultimate goal is to keep you in there. He doesn't accomplish this by telling you, "Your sinful behavior is okay." Most people in this cell already know what they're doing is wrong. Therefore, that lie wouldn't work.

What he does instead is get you so distracted by the taste of lust that you don't care about the consequences of it. In other words, Satan will give you what you want so that you can stay right where you are. The more you stay there in sin, the more desensitized you become to the Holy Spirit's conviction. When conviction goes out, more devils come in, further tightening the cords of sexual sin. But, no matter how shackled you are, or how long you've been imprisoned, there are God-given weapons that can free you!

Weapons for Freedom

I want to focus on five weapons that I believe will help you break free from Satan's prison facility.

WEAPON #1: REPENTANCE

The first mandatory weapon needed for this prison break is repentance. Without it, there is no freedom from sexual sin. Sadly, Satan has deceived our generation into thinking that repentance is just words that you say out of routine after you sin. True repentance is more than words, though. It's a change of heart and actions.

A good example of this is found in Psalm 51, when King David prayed a prayer of repentance after he committed adultery with Bathsheba and murdered her husband.

We know this was true repentance because we never hear of David ever committing adultery again. He did what repentance is supposed to do: turn you 180 degrees away from the sin and to God again. Satan is afraid of that type of repentance because it resurrects a sinner from hell's graveyard. Hell trembles at true repentance. Therefore, you must repent from your sexual sin. While doing that, you can simultaneously access weapon #2, which is confessing your sin to God and asking Him to forgive you.

WEAPON #2: CONFESS YOUR SINS TO GOD AND RECEIVE HIS FORGIVENESS.

God's forgiveness is a powerful, essential weapon for freedom. With Satan knowing this, he does everything in his power to make you feel unworthy and unable to receive God's forgiveness for your sexual sin. Thus, he'll put these thoughts of guilt, shame and self-condemnation in your head, which may sound like:

My sin is too shameful.
I don't deserve forgiveness.
God can't forgive this sin.

Because of these penetrating thoughts, many have given up and accepted their chains of defeat. They figured that if they couldn't be forgiven, why should they stop?

If only they knew, though, that these thoughts of Satan are lies and 1 John 1:9 (NKJV) says,

"If we confess our sins, He is faithful and just to forgive us our sins and to cleanse us from all unrighteousness."

All unrighteousness includes fornication, adultery, lust, homosexuality, incest, pedophilia, prostitution, pornography, rape and bestiality. There's no sexual sin that the blood of Jesus can't cleanse you from. All you have to do is confess it, and God will forgive you and make your sin of scarlet *"as white as snow"* (Isaiah 1:18, NIV). Once you've been made white as snow, it's time to pick up the next weapon that's often coupled with forgiveness, which is fasting.

> *There's no sexual sin that the blood of Jesus can't cleanse you from.*

WEAPON #3: FAST YOUR WAY OUT

Fasting is more than just turning your plate over. It's a spiritual posture to God, often done simultaneously with repentance (Joel 2:12). The end goal of fasting is to:

1. Break the yoke of sin. (Isaiah 58:6)
2. Set the oppressed free. (Isaiah 58:6)
3. Petition God to move on your behalf. (2 Samuel 12:16-22)
4. Reconnect you to God. (Joel 2:12)
5. Give you added authority over demons. (Matthew 17:21)

You need all of the above to break through the chains of lust. More specifically, fasting to get added authority over demons is essential because, on the way out of Satan's prison cell, you will need to fight his demons of lust (Satan's guards). They'll be aggressive and seductive, and they will try their hardest to keep you from leaving! In a sense, they'll feel like they own you because they've held you captive for so long. For some of these demons, it'll only be by prayer and *fasting* that you get delivered from them (Matthew 17:21). So, let's pray because today is the day that you're going to walk out of Satan's prison cell.

In the name of Jesus,

Every single demon of lust that has kept you bound must come out and leave right now. This includes:

1. The demons of lust that latched onto you as a child through molestation—we cast them out!
2. The demons that entered through an open door of pornography—we cast them out!
3. The demons that torment you with sexual dreams—we cast them out!
4. The demons that latched onto you during masturbation—we cast them out!
5. The demons of homosexuality that came onto you through curiosity or manipulation—we cast them out!
6. The demons of bestiality that came through browsing pornography—we cast them out!
7. The demons of adultery that keep you from being faithful to your spouse—we cast them out!
8. The demons of pedophilia that came through demonic curiosity—we cast them out!
9. Whatever other demon that came through whatever other open door—we cast them out and take back the authority, in the name of Jesus Christ!

Today is the day that you're going to walk out of Satan's prison cell.

Now that you've broken free from this prison cell, it's time to receive weapon #4—*the Holy Spirit*. The Holy Spirit will help navigate you out of this facility and give you the power to not return to that cell.

WEAPON #4: THE HOLY SPIRIT

After dying on the cross and raising from the grave, Jesus said these final words to His disciples concerning the Holy Spirit before He ascended to Heaven, *"You shall receive power when the Holy Spirit has come upon you"* (Acts 1:8, NKJV).

This is the same spirit and power the prophet Joel prophesied about 2800 years ago (Joel 2:28). Also, it's the same spirit the 120 (including Jesus' disciples) received in Acts 2:4 2000 years ago. Lastly, it's the same spirit that you can receive today. All you have to do is ask God for His spirit, and He will give it to you. Upon receiving His spirit, you will speak in tongues as the 120 people did in the Upper Room on the day of Pentecost. Ultimately, it's by this spirit of God, that you are given the power to stay out of that cell.

Upon receiving this power, and praying in the spirit, you'll notice an:

1. Increase in strength to walk in purity because Christ lives in you (Romans 8:10)
2. Desire to walk in purity because you're a new creature (2 Corinthians 5:17)
3. Guide to lead you into truth away from sexual sin (John 16:13)
4. Helper in your weakest and horniest moments (Romans 8:26)
5. Inward edification that removes ungodly sexual desires (1 Corinthians 14:4)

These five empowerments of the Holy Spirit are effective tools for your great escape. However, we must remember that the Holy Spirit is a helper, not an enforcer. In other words, God's spirit in you will give you the tools for this prison break, but the choice to finally break free is up to you. Nevertheless, with the Holy Spirit, this choice becomes easier because you now have the power to say, "N-O!" (weapon #5) and finally walk out of this prison facility.

WEAPON #5: N-O

Two letters that scream deliverance from this prison facility of sexual sin is N-O. You will need these two letters because as soon as Satan sees you nearing a prison break, he'll call a code red, pull out his fiercest weapons, and go to war for your soul.

I don't know about you, but every single time I got close to breaking free from this prison facility, I'd receive a tempting message. One particular moment, I had just finished reading the Word of God, and a woman sent me a naked photo. This was an attack from the enemy, hoping to keep me from freedom.

So, don't be surprised at the temptations that arise. When temptations increase, the door of freedom is right around the corner. It won't be easy to say, "No" to these temptations, especially since you'll be horny. Additionally, the enemy will be whispering these lies into your ears,

"Just do it one more time. You can repent afterward."

"You haven't done it in a few days. You'll be okay."

"You've done so good. Give yourself a little break."

If you stop and give into those lies, and taste sin one more time, that demon of lust will catch you and escort you right back to your cell. Therefore, you must reject every single temptation that tries to keep you from walking out of that prison facility. Your final, "No" to the last temptation will be the thing that breaks you through the exit doors of Satan's facility.

Once you have escaped, and gone outside, you'll finally feel the breeze of freedom and fresh air thrusting against your face. As you keep running to meet your angelic getaway car, you'll see all of the silver electric fences that enclose the millions of inmates Satan lured in. Then, as you see the demons of lust guards surrounding the facility, you'll instantly tell yourself, *I'm not ever going back there*.

As good as that sounds, and as free as you finally feel, the reality is that most prisoners eventually find their way back to that same facility. That doesn't have to be the case for you, though. You can be the success story. You can defy the odds. You can hold onto your freedom. In order to do this though, imminent changes need to be made. One of the first ones that will help you stay free upon entering into society is closing all open doors that can lead you into sexual sin.

How to Stay Free from Satan's Prison Facility

1. Close All Open Doors

These open doors may include a recent ex, old hook-up, recent sexual encounter, group of friends, seductive music, sexual movies, and anything that could tie you back to lust. It's essential that you disconnect from these people and things because all it takes is one hint of lust for you to fall into sin and be shackled all over again.

Keep this in mind, though. Closing open doors is a helpful way to keep you free, but it doesn't cancel every temptation. When a temptation does come, we must do as Joseph did, and run!

2. Run Like Joseph

Joseph was a man of God in Genesis who got tempted by Potiphar's (his boss) wife to sin sexually. This all started with Joseph being handsome and her lusting after him. One day, when she couldn't control her lust for him any longer, she told him, "Come to bed with me!" (Genesis 39:7, NIV)

As you can likely imagine, Potiphar's wife was probably naked underneath those sheets as she beckoned Joseph to come sleep with her. What made this temptation even more challenging is that Joseph was a young, *unmarried* man, given the opportunity to finally let out all of his sexual build-up.

But, would that orgasm have been worth losing his destiny? It would've felt good. But, after horniness fades away, what would he have been left with? Nothing. This means that the dreams that God gave him as a boy about him being a ruler would've never come to pass. Could you imagine the very thing you know you are destined to do not coming to pass because of one orgasm?

I believe the thoughts above went through Joseph's head as Potiphar's wife tempted him. When he considered all that he could lose, he was able to deny her advances, even to the point of running out of the house away from her.

It's going to take that same courage Joseph displayed in Genesis 39 to keep yourself out of Satan's prison. So, be ready because, when you least expect it, and when you're most vulnerable, those types of temptations will come, and you will have to run. Nevertheless, running like Joseph becomes easier when you love God with everything in you, which is the last step on how to stay free from Satan's prison cell of sexual sin.

3. Love God with Everything in You

If remaining free from this cell of sexual sin boiled down to one Bible verse, it would be, *Love the Lord your God with all your heart and with all your soul and with all your strength and with all your mind* (Luke 10:27, NIV). It's not by coincidence that it is the great commandment Jesus gives us. After all, love has the power to make you do the unimaginable.

Personally, I never imagined I could be free from Satan's facility. I was so far in sexual sin that walking out of the cell that had me chained up for almost twelve years seemed impossible. I even asked myself,

Should I just keep these chains on?
Should I just give up this fight for purity?
Should I just accept the fact that I love women, and live my life doing as I desire?

But amidst those thoughts and struggles, the Holy Ghost inside of me would never let me give up. And no matter how many nights I fell into sexual sin, God still woke me up. Although I should've woken up in hell with the smell of sulfur in my nose and smoke in my lungs, He woke me up to breathe the air of a millionth chance.

Mercy never smelled so good.

The morning sun beaming in through the window after a night of sin never felt so good. While others died in their sin, I woke up to live again.

That's love. Because of God's good merciful love toward me, I got a chance to know Him and love Him before it was too late. I didn't love Him at first because it takes time for love to grow. But after spending time in His presence, hearing His voice, and seeing Him in heaven, I now love Him with everything inside of me.

It's this love for Him that triggers faithfulness and keeps me out of Satan's prison facility. The more you love Jesus, the easier it is to be faithful to Him—even in the horniest nights. And believe me, I've had some of those nights where I desperately wanted to taste sin again. I had nights where I wrestled with demons of lust for hours on end as they tried to convince me to go back to my first love—*lust*. But,

A love for Jesus is the ultimate cure to sexual sin.

they weren't able to succeed this time because my love for Jesus outweighed anything that lust had to offer. Therefore, I can stand boldly and profess that love is the ultimate cure to sexual sin. When you love Jesus with everything in you, you will always remain free from Satan's prison cell of sexual sin.

Final Class Wrap-Up

As we approach the final moments of Christian Sex Ed., I want to let you know that Satan will do everything in his power to lock you up. If that means he has to decorate the cell full of your favorite lusts and sexual fantasies to lure you in, he'll do it.

Know this, though. If you choose to walk into that cell, one day, when you least expect it, those cell doors will shut. When they shut, your pleasure will turn into torment and you will be trapped in hell for eternity. I can only imagine how many people are in hell right now, wishing they had walked out of those cells doors before it was too late.

Don't be like them, having had countless opportunities to leave that prison cell of sexual sin, but choosing to stay in and reject the greatest gift of life, which is Jesus. Moreover, a life with Jesus is far better than any sexual pleasure. Hearing Jesus' voice, feeling His presence, and being showered with His love will always outweigh the pleasures of *any* sexual sin. So, if you're in the prison cells of sexual sin, it's time to walk out because God is ringing the bells of freedom. He is saying, "Let freedom ring! Let freedom ring!" In Jesus' name! Amen.

Thank you for finishing Christian Sex Ed!

FINAL EXAM

CHRISTIAN SEX ED FINAL EXAM

1. What percentage of Christians admitted to masturbating in the last three months?

A. 59%
B. 65%
C. 60%
D. 68%

2. Who in the Bible was given a dream from a spirit that was not of God?

A. Job
B. Lot
C. Joseph
D. Eliphaz

3. What makes masturbation sinful?

4. Who was the second couple mentioned in the Bible to have sex?

A. Abel and his wife
B. Solomon and his wife
C. Cain and his wife
D. Seth and his wife

5. What is the fourth layer of a tree trunk?

A. Sapwood
B. Wormwood
C. Heartwood
D. Cambium cell

6. What percentage of the 1000 people surveyed said that, "Sexual dreams led them into sexual sin"?

A. 49%
B. 87%
C. 76%
D. 69%

7. What percentage of Christians admitted to struggling with pornography at some point in their walk with God?

A. 62%
B. 81%
C. 61%
D. 85%

8. What invention made pornography more accessible than ever before?

9. If you want to stay free from sexual sin, what is the first step?

A. Run like Joseph.
B. Close all open doors.
C. Get an accountability partner.
D. Go on a fast.

10. Will you go to Amazon right now, and give a review of Christian Sex Ed?

A. Yes
B. Yes
C. Yes
D. Yes

CHRISTIAN SEX ED. FINAL EXAM ANSWERS

1. What percentage of Christians admitted to masturbating in the last three months?

A. 59%
B. 65%
C. 60%
D. 68%

Answer: D – 68%

2. Who in the Bible was given a dream from a spirit that was not of God?

A. Job
B. Lot
C. Joseph
D. Eliphaz

Answer: D – Eliphaz

3. What makes masturbation sinful?

Answer: Lust

4. Who was the second couple mentioned in the Bible to have sex?

A. Abel and his wife
B. Solomon and his wife
C. Cain and his wife
D. Seth and his wife

Answer: C – Cain and his wife

5. What is the fourth layer of a tree trunk?

A. Sapwood
B. Wormwood
C. Heartwood
D. Cambium cell

Answer: A – Sapwood

6. What percentage of the 1000 people surveyed said that, "Sexual dreams led them into sexual sin"?

A. 49%
B. 87%
C. 76%
D. 69%

Answer: C – 76%.

7. What percentage of Christians admitted to struggling with pornography at some point in their walk with God?

A. 62%
B. 81%
C. 61%
D. 85%

Answer: D – 85%

8. What invention made pornography more accessible than ever before?

Answer: The Internet

9. If you want to stay free from sexual sin, what is the first step?

A. Run like Joseph.
B. Close all open doors.
C. Get an accountability partner.
D. Go on a fast.

Answer: B – Close all open doors.

10. Will you go to Amazon right now, and give a review of Christian Sex Ed?

A. Yes
B. Yes
C. Yes
D. Yes

Answer: A through D.

If you answered at least seven questions correctly, then you received a credit for this semester. Congratulations.

ABOUT THE AUTHOR

Dane Fragger is the founder of Christian Sex Ed. Ministries. Millions of believers around the world who desire to learn about dating, sex, and sexual purity view his content each month. Over the last couple of years, Dane has been interviewed on national television and by several highly esteemed radio stations and podcasts.

He holds a bachelor's degree in Psychology and is working towards a master's degree in Biblical Studies. He is also a graduate from Word of Life Bible Institute. Dane has been in ministry for eight years and currently serves as a pastor on staff in Los Angeles, California, where he lives with his beautiful wife, Asia, and lovely daughters, Eliana and Elizabeth.

FOR MORE INFORMATION, VISIT:

www.DaneFragger.com
Instagram: @ChristianSexEd
Facebook: @ChristianSexEd
YouTube: @ChristianSexEd
Instagram: @danefragger

If you've enjoyed this book, please leave a review on Amazon!

ALSO BY DANE FRAGGER:

Young and Saved: Living In a World That's Not Like You

CHRISTIAN SEX ED. GLOSSARY

ADULTERY: Sexual intercourse outside of marriage by one or both parties.

COGNITIVE BEHAVIORAL THERAPY (CBT): A common psychotherapy used to treat someone who is struggling with sexual addiction. The goal of this therapy is to help individuals find out what is triggering their sexual behaviors. Furthermore, CBT helps individuals stop engaging in compulsive sexual behaviors by finding healthy outlets.

FOREPLAY: Sexual acts of touching and kissing between two individuals prior to sex.

FORNICATION: Sexual intercourse between two people that aren't married to each other or pre-marital sex.

LUST (SINFUL): Broadly defined, lust is: a very strong desire for someone or something, generally of a sexual nature. That definition doesn't completely capture the lust that the Bible condemns. (See Job 31:1; Proverbs 6:25; Matthew 5:28; Romans 1:26–27). The sinful lust that the Bible warns us against can also be defined as the sexual coveting or objectification of someone that you're not married to. Additionally, sexual desires become sinful lust when they *willfully* manifest through the eyes, imaginations, thoughts, actions, and the heart with the intent to gain sexual gratification. In other words, the only person that you can *willfully* think about or look at in a way that brings you *sexual gratification* is your spouse of the opposite sex.

NOTE: Throughout this book, the terms "sinful lust" and "lust" are used interchangeably.

MASTURBATION: The act of using your hands, or an object, on your genitals for sexual pleasure.

PORNOGRAPHY: Sexually explicit magazines, photographs and videos that intend to arouse one sexually. These pornographic items often include nudity, acts of sex, group orgies and other erotic behaviors.

SEX ADDICTION (OR HYPERSEXUALITY): Sex addiction is when a person loses control over their sexual behaviors and has become dependent on excessive amounts of sexual activity, in spite of the negative outcomes that follow. Furthermore, you know it's addiction when the individual must engage in high amounts of sexual activity to flee from the feelings of *withdrawal*, which is the first symptom of addiction.

SEXUAL DREAMS: Dreams of a sexual nature that can include you having sex, watching sex, pursuing sex, and/or reliving past sexual experiences.

SEXUAL IMMORALITY: Sexual acts that violate God's rules for sex (e.g., adultery, fornication, homosexuality, bestiality).

SEXUAL INTERCOURSE (SEX): When a male puts his erected penis into a woman's vagina. At the peak of this intercourse, orgasms can take place, in which a man ejaculates semen and a woman has a release of sexual pressure, which comes with her vagina, anus and uterus contracting. Women can ejaculate, as well.

WET DREAMS: When an individual dreams about something sexual, while involuntarily ejaculating fluid from his or her genitals, without masturbation.

END NOTES

1. Thayer, Joseph Henry. *A Greek–English Lexicon of the New Testament*. New York: Harper & Brothers, 1889 pp.79-80.

CPSIA information can be obtained
at www.ICGtesting.com
Printed in the USA
BVHW071105021220
594678BV00004B/639